My Dog Tulip

J. R. ACKERLEY

POSEIDON PRESS

NEW YORK

Copyright © 1965 by J. R. Ackerley
All rights reserved
including the right of reproduction
in whole or in part in any form

Published by Poseidon Press,
A Division of Simon & Schuster, Inc.
Simon & Schuster Building
Rockefeller Center
1230 Avenue of the Americas
New York, New York 10020
Published by arrangement with Fleet Press
POSEIDON PRESS is a registered trademark of
Simon & Schuster, Inc.

Designed by Eve Metz
Manufactured in the United States of America
1 3 5 7 9 10 8 6 4 2

Library of Congress Cataloging in Publication Data
Ackerley, J. R. (Joe Randolph), 1896-1967.
My dog Tulip.
Reprint. Originally published: New York : Fleet, 1965.
1. Ackerley, J. R. (Joe Randolph), 1896-1967—
Biography. 2. Authors, English—20th century—Biography.
3. Dog owners—Great Britain—Biography. 4. German
shepherd dogs—Biography. 5. Dogs—Great Britain—
Biography. I. Title.
PR6001.C4Z468   1987   828'.91203   [B]   86-20474
ISBN 0-671-63471-2

Contents

1 · The Two Tulips

*S*ome years ago, when I was walking with my dog in Fulham Palace Gardens, we overtook an old woman who was wheeling a baby carriage. She was chatting cheerfully to the occupant of it, and it was therefore, perhaps, not unreasonable of me to be surprised to find, when I caught up with her, that this too was a dog. He was lying upon his back, propped up by pillows, with a rug tucked round his middle; just above the top of the rug the edge of a thick bandage was visible. Very comfortable and peaceful the little dog looked as the old woman trundled him along among the flowers, chatting to him in that bright, encouraging way in which people address invalids.

I made some sympathetic remark to her as I passed, and she was all agog to tell me about her troubles, how the poor little dog had been so seriously ill with an internal tumor, but how he was well on the road to recovery now, thanks, oh thanks—she could not thank her enough—to the wonderful lady vet who had operated on him and been so clever and so kind, for had it not been for her, the little dog, who was such a good little dog, would undoubtedly have died.

'Wouldn't you, love?' said she to the invalid, who lay back motionless against the pillows, with his paws folded on his stomach and a very solemn expression on his small pointed face.

This conversation made a deep impression upon me. I was then quite new to the dog world, for my present dog was the first I had ever possessed, and there was much that I did not know and wished to learn. It astounded me to hear that dogs underwent major operations and had their stomachs opened and shut as we do, and I tried to picture this little mongrel lying upon the operating table, under the glare of the head-lamps, with the grave faces of surgeons, nurses, and anaesthetists bent over him. What on earth would happen to my dog, I wondered uneasily, if she should ever develop anything so serious as an internal tumor? Who would care to operate on her? Before parting from the old woman, I did not fail to take the name and address of the lady vet who had been 'so clever and so kind.'

My own dog is an Alsatian bitch. Her name is Tulip. Alsatians have a bad reputation; they are said to bite the hand that feeds them. Indeed Tulip bit my hand once, but accidentally; she mistook it for a rotten apple we were both trying to grab simultaneously. One of her canines sank into my thumb-joint to the bone: when I held it under the tap afterwards I could see the sinews exposed. We all make mistakes and she was dreadfully sorry. She rolled over on the grass with all her legs in the air; and later on, when she saw the bandage on my hand, she put herself in the corner, the darkest corner of the bedroom, and stayed there for the rest of the afternoon. One can't do more than that.

But if you look like a wild beast you are expected to behave like one; and human beings, who tend to disregard the savagery of their own conduct, shake their heads over the Alsatian dog. 'What can you expect of a wolf?' they say.*

Tulip made no conspicuous effort to improve this situation. If people were inclined to look at her askance she gave them every reason to do so. They distrusted her; she suspected them. In fact she repudiated the human

* 'Don't let that dog near me!' shouted a tramp to me one day on Brook Green. 'They ain't to be trusted!'
'You don't look particularly trustworthy yourself,' I replied, and might be thought to have hit a nail on the head, for he at once fumbled a jack-knife out of his miscellaneous garments and, opening it with some difficulty, flourished it after me.

race altogether—that is to say the remainder of it. *I* could do with her whatever I wished—except stop her barking at other people. In this matter, she seemed to say, she knew better than I. Yet she behaved always with exemplary dignity and good breeding wherever she went, so long as she was let alone: it was when anyone approached her, or even gave the impression of being about to approach her, that she spoke her mind. She spoke sharply and loud, and she had a good deal to say, though what precisely her mind was I did not know. In truth, although I was very anxious to know, I was less anxious to find out. Her sweetness and gentleness to myself were such that it was almost impossible for me to believe that these were not the prevailing characteristics of her nature; but the language she used to others certainly sounded pretty strong, and bad language, as is well known, does not always stop at that.

No doubt the reason why I took the constant care I did take to protect her from being put to the test of showing how far she would go, was that I had to admit I had an inkling; but the two bus conductors and the postman whom she had already bitten could hardly be accepted as a true sociological sample of her feelings for mankind. They had all been doing things, like coming soundlessly upon us in sneakers, or striking the bus a sudden sharp rat-tat alongside us with their ticket racks to make it move on, of which it is in the nature of dogs to disapprove; in any case she had not hurt them, but merely taken them by the sleeve or by the arm; and though one of the conductors had rolled back his cuff to display the wound, he himself seemed disappointed that there was nothing to be seen but a small white dent in his flesh.

When children are called difficult the cause is often

traced to their homes, and it was upon Tulip's first home that I blamed her unsociable conduct. She had originally belonged to some working-class people who, though fond of her in their way, seldom took her out. She was too excitable, and too valuable, to be allowed off the leash; on it she pulled. For nearly a year she scarcely left their house, but spent her time, mostly alone, for they were at work all day, in a tiny backyard. She could hardly be expected, therefore, to learn the ways of a world she so rarely visited; the only 'training' she ever received was an occasional thrashing for the destruction which her owners discovered when they returned home. Alsatians in particular do not take kindly to beatings; they are too intelligent and too nervous. It was from this life, when she was eighteen months old, that I rescued her, and to it that I attributed the disturbances of her psyche. Thereafter it was clear that if she could have her way she would never let me out of her sight again.

It is necessary to add that she is beautiful. People are always wanting to touch her, a thing she cannot bear. Her ears are tall and pointed, like the ears of Anubis. How she manages to hold them constantly erect, as though starched, I do not know, for with their fine covering of mouse-gray fur they are soft and flimsy; when she stands with her back to the sun it shines through the delicate tissue, so that they glow shell-pink as though incandescent. Her face also is long and pointed, basically stone-gray but the snout and lower jaw are jet black. Jet, too, are the rims of her amber eyes, as though heavily mascara'd, and the tiny mobile eyebrow tufts that are set like accents above them. And in the midst of her forehead is a kind of Indian caste-mark, a black diamond suspended there, like the jewel on the brow of Pegasus in Mantegna's 'Parnassus,' by a fine dark thread, no more than a pencilled line, which is drawn from it right over her poll midway between the tall ears. A shadow extends across her forehead from either side of this caste-mark, so that, in certain lights, the diamond looks like the body of a bird with its wings spread, a bird in flight.

These dark markings symmetrically divide up her face into zones of pale pastel colors, like a mosaic, or a stained-glass window; her skull, bisected by the thread, is two primrose pools, the center of her face light gray, the bridge of her nose above the long, black lips fawn, her cheeks white, and upon each a *patte de mouche* has been tastefully set. A delicate white ruff, frilling out from the lobes of her ears, frames this strange, clownish face, with its heavily leaded features, and covers the whole of her throat and chest with a snowy shirt front.

For the rest, her official description is sable-gray: she is a gray dog wearing a sable tunic. Her gray is the gray of birch bark; her sable tunic is of the texture of satin and clasps her long body like a saddle-cloth. No tailor could have shaped it more elegantly; it is cut round the joints of her shoulders and thighs and in a straight line along the points of her ribs, lying open at the chest and stomach. Over her rump it fits like a cap, and then extends on in a thin strip over the top of her long tail down to the tip. Viewed from above, therefore, she is a black dog; but when she rolls over on her back she is a gray one. Two dark ribbons of fur, descending from her tunic over her shoulders, fasten it at her sternum, which seems to clip the ribbons together as with an ivory brooch.

She had been to three vets already for various reasons.

It was a measure of my naïveté in dog affairs that my first consultation with a vet was to inquire whether she was in heat. The question was never settled, that is to say by him, for when he was finally able to make himself heard, in his bleak surgery, above her deafening challenge and my own vain exhortations to her to calm herself, all he said, in a cold voice, was, 'Have you any control over your dog?'

In the face of the evidence it seemed idle to return anything but 'No'; to which, still keeping his distance, he drily replied, 'Then take her out of my surgery at once.'

Some weeks later she sustained a small cut in one of her pads, which took so long to heal that I began to fear that it would never heal at all; another vet had been recommended to me, and I decided to try my luck with him. He was an ex-Army man, a Major, and the most that I asked of Tulip on this occasion was that she should allow me to flex her paw so that, without touching her, he could glance at the cut. But she would not permit even that. Having failed, as I had failed, to humor her or shout her down, the Major suddenly lost his temper, and exclaiming, 'These Alsatians! They're all the same!' he swooped upon her and beat her about the body with his bare hands.

These dashing military tactics were not without effect; they drove her, trembling with astonishment and fear, beneath his operating table, from the shelter of which she looked out at him with an expression which I might secretly excuse but could not approve; but they did not enable him to examine her, if that was part of his plan, and they could hardly be construed as an invitation to call again. They implied also, I took it, a rebuke to myself, as well as the more obvious one they meted out to her; they were teaching me a much needed lesson in how to discipline an unruly dog: 'Spare the rod and spoil the child!' was what the Major was, in effect, saying.

As I walked away from this establishment with Tulip, who was now in her gayest and most winning mood, I supposed myself to be in possession of an undoctorable dog; but this gloomy reflection was succeeded by two others of a more comforting nature. The first was that, after all, she hadn't bitten the Major. And he might truly be said to have asked for that. Flinging caution to the winds, he had set about her; but she had not retaliated: whatever savagery had been exhibited in the surgery had not been exhibited by her. My other reflection was, in one way, even more comforting. 'These Alsatians! They're all the same!' he had said. Tulip, then, was not exceptional in her tiresomeness. She was not, so to speak, a delinquent dog. If all Alsatians were the same, her peculiarities were of the breed and not an individual affair. But if all Alsatians were the same, did any of them ever receive medical attention?

It transpired that they did; and above all the conflicting emotions that rent me when we visited our third vet—this time for a most important service, to have her inoculated against distemper—was gratitude that he did not summon the police or the fire department. I had made the appointment by telephone, and had thought it politic to apologise for Tulip in advance and to explain that, although I did not believe there was really any harm in her, she was not the most amenable of patients. To this the vet had merely grunted: when I set out with her I was already unnerved by the thought of the struggle that lay ahead. Nor were my drooping spirits raised by the first sight that greeted us, a Spaniel who was being treated as we arrived. This creature was visible to us, like some callous admonishment, before ever we reached the surgery door, for its window looked out upon a yard through which we had to pass, and the Spaniel was all too plainly seen within.

He was standing quietly on a table with a thermometer sticking out of his bottom, like a cigarette. And this humiliating spectacle was rendered all the more crushing by the fact that there was no one else there. Absolutely motionless, and with an air of deep absorption, the dog was standing upon the table in an empty room with a thermometer in his bottom, almost as though he had put it there himself.

'Oh, Tulip!' I groaned. 'If only you were like that!'

But she was not. When the vet returned from his dispensary and, the thermometer and the spaniel having been successively removed, was free to turn his attention to us, she was not in the least like that. Suspecting the place's character, no doubt, from the pervasive odor of medicaments and the howls and moans of the various sick animals penned in the kennel at the back, she had exhibited the strongest aversion to entering it, and was now imploring and cajoling me to take her away: as soon as the vet opened his mouth to speak, she replied. A gray little man with an unsmiling face, he stood with his syringe in his hand patiently waiting while I petted and coaxed poor Tulip, speaking soothingly to her in baby language, as she shrank, dribbled, and barked between my knees.

'Can you turn her back to me and hold her head still?' he inquired, in a momentary lull.

'I think so,' I said nervously.

But to turn her back on this odious little man was the last thing that Tulip intended; she squirmed convulsively out of my grasp over and over again, eventually wrenching her head out of her collar. Under the vet's expressionless gaze I had to retrieve her and rebuckle it, with hands which, he probably noticed, shook as much as she did.

'May I give her the injection myself?' I asked. 'You could show me where to do it and she wouldn't mind it from me.'

The vet made no reply. Instead, he laid his syringe upon the table, rang the bell, selected a strip of bandage from a hook on the wall and made a loop in it—all without a word. The door opened, and an assistant came in.

'Good!' exclaimed the vet to me, with sudden briskness. 'Now just keep her head like that for a moment!' and advancing the loop towards Tulip, who was still determinedly pointing her face at him, and now glared at the approaching contraption as though mesmerised, he abruptly noosed her nose, with what was plainly the dexterity of long practice, drew her jaws tightly and roughly together, turned the ends of the tape round her throat and knotted them behind her ears.

'Oh, I say!' I cried. 'Don't hurt her! There's really no need.'

I was, indeed, in no position, or even mind, to question whatever methods this busy and helpful man might think fit to employ to exercise over my animal the control I lacked, and my miserable ejaculation was only wrung from me by the sight of Tulip's horror-stricken face and the squawk of pain and despair she uttered before her powers of speech were cut rudely short.

My thoughts, in fact, were in the utmost confusion. I

suffered to see my dear, affectionate dog ill-used, but I could hardly expect my tender feelings to be shared by a vet who was meeting her for the first time and clearly did not bring out in her, like myself, the sweetest and the best. What should I do, I pondered, if I were in his shoes, confronted with a strange, large, vulpine, and unfriendly dog, possessed of an excellent set of teeth, into whom I was asked to stick a needle? Would I cheer-fully grasp her with hands upon the wholeness of which my means of livelihood depended? Yet, on the other side, could it be good for a creature, already so nervous and mistrustful, to be subjected to such violent stratagems?

However, for all the attention the vet paid me, I might never have spoken. 'Now, Bob!' was all he said, and, brushing me aside, he and his assistant took hold of the defenceless Tulip, who was foaming at the mouth with terror, and pulling her legs from beneath her, brought her heavily to the ground.

'Pass the syringe,' said the vet.

After this, my ambition in life was to keep Tulip in such a state of health that she need never visit a vet again. It was an ambition which she herself appeared to share. She would not, if she could help it, even enter the streets in which her last two experiences had taken place. If I happened to forget and turned down one of them when we were out, I would suddenly miss her from my side, an unheard-of thing, and looking wildly round, espy her far behind me, motionless at the corner, star-ing after me with her exclamation-mark face. There is no getting away from Tulip's face; with its tall ears con-stantly focused upon one it demands an attention which it seems unremittingly to give. She fixes one, as one is sometimes claimed and fixed by those insistent bores who, when they have something to impart, hold one's gaze with a searching, inescapable stare, as though they know from experience that the attention of their listeners is apt to wander and are determined to exact that responsive gleam of intelligence which their remorseless personalities require. 'Are you listening?' they say, irritably or plaintively, from time to time.

Tulip's face perpetually said the same thing, for with all its perpendicular lines, the tall ears, the long nose, the black streak down the forehead and the little vertical eyebrow tufts, it was not merely interrogatory but exclamatory also: it said both 'What?' and 'What!' Useless to call her now, she would not budge; I must return to her and reach my objective by another route; but later I discovered that she would consent to follow me down these unsavory roads so long as I reassured her, by passing the surgeries, that it was not my intention to enter them. Then she would come, but always with infinite distaste, crossing the road to make the widest possible detour and hurrying past the baleful buildings, casting at them every now and then a repugnant, sidelong glance.

But my disinclination to visit vets was in frequent conflict with my need to consult them; perplexities of all sorts troubled my ignorant and anxious mind, and not the least of my worries at the time of my encounter with the old woman in Fulham Palace Gardens was that, in spite of the nourishing food I provided, Tulip looked too thin; beneath her sable tunic all her ribs were visible. The distressing word 'Worms' was dropped into my ear by a kind acquaintance, and soon afterwards I decided to take her along to see Miss Canvey, which was the name of the lady vet who had been 'so clever and so kind.' Her surgery was in Parsons Green, and to the kennel maid who answered the phone I explained, in the apologetic manner which was now habitual with me, that my bitch was very difficult and I would prefer, if convenient, to bring her along out of surgery hours.

Miss Canvey was a short, thickset, young woman with bobbed hair, spectacles, and a homely peasant's face. She wore a white overall, not intimidatingly clean, and as she advanced across the large, bare room towards me, I took an impression of calmness and competence. I had spoken sternly to Tulip as we waited, exhorting her to good behavior for a change, but I had no expectation of any improvement and there was none; she accorded Miss Canvey her usual defiant reception—defiance which became the more emphatic the more it was ignored. Miss Canvey approached imperturbably and stood quietly in front of us, looking down at her, while I stumbled through some account of her past and present troubles, punctuated with irritable commands to the dog to pipe down.

'She's like this with everyone,' I said ruefully, 'but as sweet as pie to me. I can't make it out.'

Miss Canvey did not speak, but continued to gaze down at the excited animal. Then she asked:

'What's her name?' I told her. 'Well Tulip, you *are* a noisy girl, aren't you? What's it all about?' and she extended her hand, back foremost. Tulip paused for a moment to sniff it, then, as the hand was moved closer, retreated, barking more violently than ever. How maddening, how intolerable it was that this creature, usually so attentive and obedient to my wishes, should always let me down in public in this stupid way! Suddenly yell-ing 'Stop it, you brute!' I biffed her on the nose. The blow was harder than I intended. Tulip gave a little cry of pain and rubbed her nose with her paw. Then she rose up on her hind legs and gently licked my face.

'I see,' said Miss Canvey promptly. 'You're the trouble.'

'I?' I exclaimed, astonished.

'Just slip the lead through her collar, will you. I'll examine her in another room.'

'Are you sure it will be all right?' I asked anxiously, doing as I was bid.

'Perfectly all right.' And twisting the lead round her strong wrist, she marched firmly out of the room, towing behind her the horrified and struggling Tulip who cast back at me agonized glances as she slid and sprawled across the linoleum. The door closed.

Alone in the surgery I listened apprehensively for sounds—screams from Miss Canvey, cries of pain or rage from Tulip, rushing feet, banging doors—sounds of any sort: none could be reassuring. But the place was as silent as the grave. Then, after what seemed an eternity but was only ten minutes, I heard a scuffling in the passage and a few barks, but of a very different timbre; the door opened and Tulip reappeared, this time with Miss Canvey in tow.

'No sign of worms,' remarked the latter, dropping the lead. 'She's in excellent condition.'

'How did she behave?' I asked, while Tulip cast herself into my arms and lavished upon me a greeting more suitable in its extravagance to lovers who had been parted for years.

'Good as gold,' said Miss Canvey.

'Did you tie up her nose?'

'Heavens, no! I never do that.'

'But you had help?' I said, gazing mistily at her.

Miss Canvey smiled:

'Of course not. She was no trouble. I knew she wouldn't be.'

'How did you know?' I asked humbly.

'Well, you learn by experience, I suppose. But it isn't difficult to tell a dog's character from its face. Tulip's a good girl, I saw that at once. You're the trouble.'

I sat down.

'Do tell me,' I said.

'Well, she's in love with you, that's obvious. And so life's full of worries for her. She has to protect you to begin with; that's why she's upset when people approach you: I expect she's a bit jealous, too. But in order to protect you she's naturally got to be free; that's why she doesn't like other people touching her; she's afraid, you see, that they may take hold of her and deprive her of her freedom to guard you. That's all the fuss is about, I should say. It's you she's thinking of. But when you're not there, there's nothing for her to do, of course, and no anxiety. Anyone can handle her then. I'm sure. That's all,' she concluded with a smile. 'Dog's aren't difficult to understand. One has to put oneself in their position.'

Miss Canvey could have put herself in any position she wished, for I was already her slave and gazed at her with the veneration with which we behold a saint. I asked her some questions about Tulip's diet, paid the fee—half-a-crown, so far as I recall, was all that this miracle cost—and took my leave. As I was going, she suddenly said:

'Why do you shout at her?'

'I don't know,' I stammered, rather taken aback. 'She

exasperates me sometimes. She doesn't seem to hear
what I say.'

'She can hear a pin drop!' said Miss Canvey briefly.
'Look at her ears!' Then on a milder note: 'Try not to.
It's bad for her. She's very highly strung. Speak to her
quietly; she'll do anything you want in time.'

As we walked away I apologised to Tulip for hitting
her on her beautiful nose, and, in my thoughts, for much
else besides. In the light of Miss Canvey's interpretation,
how infinitely more hideous that abject struggle in the
last vet's surgery now seemed, how heroic her conduct,
how mean and contemptible mine. I had apologised for
her devotion, and then betrayed it. I recollected, with a
shudder, how I had held her head still for the approaching trap. I felt very tender towards her.

After this, we may be said almost to have lived in the
surgery of dear Miss Canvey, that Florence Nightingale
of the animal world. I walked Tulip over to see her on
any pretext, however trifling, and such was the confidence she inspired that very soon I no longer bothered
to make special appointments, but dropped in during
surgery hours and sat with Tulip in the crowded room
awaiting our turn and watching wonderful Miss Canvey
at work upon a miscellaneous assortment of sick dogs,
cats, rabbits, and poultry. It was an enthralling and up-
lifting spectacle, and though her white overalls became
less and less white and her bobbed hair more and more
disordered, she never lost that air of calm authority
which it was a positive tonic to breathe. That Tulip ever
enjoyed these visits as much as I did, I cannot pretend;
but my own freedom from anxiety no doubt affected her
too; what resistance she put up seemed more perfunctory, and once inside, she sat by my knee quietly, except

for an occasional mew of impatience, until her turn came. Then, of course, when the solid little figure of Miss Canvey approached us, she put on her act, though with less of the old conviction; with a genial word of welcome, Miss Canvey simply took the lead and towed her from the room.

One day I observed among the other pilgrims to this shrine a young working man with his Collie dog, which was muzzled. Miss Canvey was busily engaged in extracting a tintack from the anus of a hen, and it was some time before she noticed him. Then she called across the room:

'Why is your dog muzzled?'

'I don't trust 'im, Miss,' said the young man, blushing.

'Take it off,' said Miss Canvey.

She always spoke quietly, though sometimes, as now, rather abruptly; no one ever thought of disobeying her, and the young man complied. When his turn came she examined his dog with her usual coolness and thoroughness; then she took the young man aside and spoke earnestly to him in a corner. I could not catch what she said, but at the end of it he smiled and murmured 'Thank you, Miss.' Then he went off with his dog, carrying the muzzle in his hand.

While this little scene was being enacted, I happened to be sitting near the desk where Miss Canvey's kennel-maid was writing out prescriptions, and leaning over, I whispered to her:

'Has Miss Canvey ever been bitten?'

The kennel-maid looked cautiously round before replying; then she said, in a low, hesitant voice:

'Well, she has once, to my knowledge; but I don't think she'd like it known.'

'Please tell me.'

'I didn't actually see it happen,' said the girl, 'because I was busy with something else; but I heard a sort of scuffle—it was another Collie she was treating, too—and saw her go quickly out of the room holding her hand. When she returned she had a bandage on her wrist, but she went back to finish what she'd been doing. I asked, "Did he bite you?" but all she said, rather shortly, was "It was my fault. I was clumsy." And though I offered to take over the case from her, and so did Mr. Mather when he got to hear of it, she would never let anyone else handle the dog all the time he was ill. He never hurt her again, and they became very good friends in the end.'

'Sublime woman!' I said.

The kennel-maid smiled:

'She's fond of animals, and so they like and trust her. All animals, but specially horses. They're what she likes best.'

Alas, it was true. She loved horses more than dogs, and so I have to speak of her in the past tense, for after we had enjoyed less than a year of her ministrations, her true love galloped her away into a country practice. Happy the horses wherever she is! But my own spirits went into the deepest mourning. Miss Canvey herself, I think, experienced a certain sense of guilt at abandoning us. Looking into my downcast face for the last time, she said:

'I'm not exceptional, you know.'

'You are to me,' I said, with a sigh.

Flushing a little, she said firmly:

'You can tell any vet from me that Tulip is perfectly

all right. But she must always be examined away from you. It's you who cause the trouble. Tell them that. She's a nervous bitch, and you make her more nervous. But when you're out of the way anyone can handle her. You can tell them all that from me.'

Then she uttered the last words I was ever to hear from her lips, and which, although I was too stunned by the sickening blow they dealt me to take in their full implication at the time, afforded me, in retrospect, a glimpse, the most revealing I ever had, into the depths of her heart. Fixing me with a significant look, she said:

'Never let anyone feed Tulip but yourself!'

Dear Miss Canvey, she was a romantic, of course; yet with her rather matter-of-fact air of sturdy capability she managed to convey a quite different impression, and it was only after she had gone that I was able to perceive how profoundly romantic she was. Indeed, if she had stayed, I might never have perceived it at all, for how should I have known that the two different dogs she insisted upon my possessing, the Tulip who lived always at my side, and that other Tulip with whom she had made herself privately familiar, were, to all intents and purposes, the same? This concept of hers, in fact, that I was guarded by an unapproachable tigress who became, in my absence, the meekest of lambs, had almost everything to recommend it; it worked and it pleased; it enchanted me, and so far as Miss Canvey herself was concerned, it appealed, I feel sure, to something so deep in her nature that I believe she might have gone to almost any lengths to keep the two Tulips apart. Moreover, a bewitching air of mystery enwrapped it; a transformation rite had to be performed, with Miss Canvey as High Priestess, and an act of faith was required on both sides;

for just as I could never know Miss Canvey's Tulip except by repute, since she existed only in my absence, so it was an essential part of Miss Canvey's programme that she also must take—or rather leave—my Tulip for granted.

This may sound fanciful; but how else can her last terrible injunction be explained unless on the grounds that she wished to perpetuate the romantic situation which she herself had created and cherished, and which, she divined, satisfied in me, too, some profound psychological need? How truly those last insidious words found their mark! For I could not feed Tulip myself! I was too busy, and such offices, as Miss Canvey herself knew, were already in process of being delegated to a housekeeper, lately engaged for the purpose. Had I made a ghastly mistake? Was I now about to lose my Tulip, that savage lover and protector whom Miss Canvey had striven so hard to preserve for me intact? Should I find myself soon with Miss Canvey's Tulip, that reduced, spiritless, abject creature, anybody's stroke, while my housekeeper enjoyed the fierce flattery of mine? That this obsessive fear haunted my life for many months was proof enough how well Miss Canvey had sized me up. But—she would be the first to rejoice— she had not sized up Tulip. Indeed, how should human beings suspect in the lower beasts those noblest virtues which they themselves attain only in the realms of fiction? Tulip was incorruptible. She was constant. It mattered not who fed, flattered, or befriended her, or for how long; her allegiance never wavered; she had given her heart to me in the beginning, and mine, and mine only, it was to remain forever.

Miss Canvey therefore underrated her, and it was left

to Mr. Brasenose of Brighton to whom I next had re-
course for veterinary aid—Tulip's nails needed cutting—
to imply that she had overrated her too. Mr. Brasenose
was a cheerful young man who whistled while he
worked, who continued to whistle, indeed, throughout
Tulip's customary hostilities, and when I had recited to
him Miss Canvey's magic formula, which I had learnt
by heart, all he said was:

'Oh, I shouldn't bother to go. I expect Tulip would
prefer you to stay.'

This was so far from being an aspect of the matter
that had occurred to me, that it needed a moment or two
to take it in; by the time I had focused it and, as it
seemed to me, its total and reckless wrongheadedness, he
had got his clippers out and was saying, 'Just hoist her
on the table, will you?' in so casual a manner, as though
she were a sack, that I found myself complying. The
operation was not performed without difficulty; Mrs.
Brasenose, indeed, had to be summoned by her husband
from an inner apartment to help me prop Tulip up on
the table and retrieve those various portions of her anat-
omy which, like the fringes of a jelly on too small a
plate, kept escaping over the edge; but at any rate it was
performed, by the merrily trilling vet, and with as little
concern for Tulip's protests and struggles as if he had
been cutting the nails of a mouse.

Thus opened another chapter of Tulip's medical history, and the last; although I continued faithfully to repeat my formula to all the vets we subsequently visited,
none of them paid to it the least attention. This strange
heedlessness upset me at first; not on their account, of
course; if they chose to ignore Miss Canvey's advice,
that was their lookout; but was it fair to Tulip to impose

on her this additional strain of worrying about me when she had trouble enough of her own? Upon reflection, however, I was less sure; since the ruling passion of her life was to keep me always in her eye, might she not actually prefer me to stay?

Moreover, this new chapter, I gradually perceived, had one considerable advantage; it shed light upon the problem that had embarrassed my public life with Tulip from the start and which Miss Canvey had deliberately left unexplored: What was my Tulip really like? How far, in my presence, would she go? It turned out that she was Miss Canvey's Tulip—that is to say 'as good as gold.' This was what I had always believed, and what Miss Canvey herself had seemed to confirm when she said that she saw at a glance that Tulip was a 'good girl'—leaving, however, unclear in my mind to what lengths, in Miss Canvey's philosophy, a good girl might be permitted to go in defence of her man, or her horse.

Tulip was a good girl; but as I went on hoisting her up on to one surgery table after another and supporting her there while the vets took swabs of her womb, or, opening her scissor-like jaws with their bare hands, rammed yards of stomach-pump tubing down her throat, I experienced, besides gratitude and admiration for her self-restraint, a kind of nostalgia for the past. Life was becoming dull and prosaic; something had gone out of it with dear Miss Canvey, some enrichment, some fine flavor. And this, I then knew, was the very knowledge from which, in her wisdom, she had sought to protect me: the death of the legend, the disillusionment of the heart. My Tulip: had it not now to be admitted that she had been seen through, that her bluff had been called, her stature reduced? No tigress she, but—must I face it?—an ordinary dog. Was it not even possible that, in the course of time, under these civilizing processes, she would become so tame, so characterless, so commonplace, that she might one day be found standing in a surgery alone with a thermometer in her bottom?

Tulip never let me down. She is nothing if not consistent. She knows where to draw the line, and it is always in the same place, a circle around us both. Indeed, she is a good girl, but—and this is the point—she would not care for it to be generally known. So wherever Miss Canvey may be—jogging, I hope, down some leafy lane upon a steed who will let no one mount him but herself—I would like her to know that Tulip is still the kind of good girl of whom she would approve. When, therefore, the little local boys ask me, as they often do, in their respectful and admiring way, though mistaking Tulip's gender: 'Does he bite, Mister?' I always return the answer which she, and Miss Canvey, would wish me to give.

2 · Liquids and Solids

*I*n the Journal of General Bertrand,* Napoleon's Grand Marshal at St. Helena, the entry occurs: '1821, April 12: At ten-thirty the Emperor passed a large and

* *Napoleon at St. Helena.* Memoirs of General Bertrand, Grand Marshal of the Palace. January to May, 1821. Translated by Frances Hume (Cassell).

well-formed motion.' I am not greatly interested in Napoleon's motions, but I sympathize with General Bertrand nevertheless, for Tulip's cause me similar concern. Indeed, whereas the Emperor's were probably of only *a posteriori* interest to persons other than himself—that is to say during ill-health—hers require constant supervision. The reason for this is that she has two small anal glands, which Napoleon did not have. These canine glands produce a secretion which is automatically expressed by the passage of a well-formed motion. If, however, a dog is being unsuitably fed, or, from some other cause, is continually loose in its bowels, the glands become congested and are liable to form abscesses. Tulip herself, so wilful over diet, developed trouble of this kind; but luckily a penicillin injection put it right. Another dog of my acquaintance had to undergo a severe anal operation from which, although he lived for some time after, he never completely recovered and died at last of a hemorrhage. When it is remembered that dogs express their emotions by moving their tails, it will be readily understood that the aftermath of such an operation must be extremely painful and the surgical wounds difficult to heal.

These prefatory remarks may help to extenuate the vulgar brawl that took place some years ago on the Embankment at Putney, which is the name of the riverside street below my flat. It was a misty September morning, and I had taken Tulip out at about 8:30 to relieve herself. This she was peacefully doing on the sidewalk beneath the plane trees, while I stood anxiously observing her nearby. She too seldom produced at this period the kind of motions that General Bertrand describes. But apart from my interest in the results, it always pleases me to see her perform this physical act. She lowers herself carefully and gradually to a tripodal attitude with her hind legs splayed and her heels as far apart as she can get them so as not to soil her fur or her feet. Her long tail, usually carried aloft in a curve, stretches rigidly out parallel with the ground; her ears lie back, her head cranes forward, and a mild, meditative look settles on her face.

While we were thus harmlessly engaged in the otherwise empty road, a cyclist shot round the corner of the Star and Garter Hotel towards us, pedalling rapidly. He was a youngish man, wearing a rather dirty raincoat. Since Tulip was safely on the sidewalk, I don't suppose I should have noticed this person at all if he had not addressed me as he flew past:

'Try taking your dog off the sidewalk to mess!'

One should not lose one's temper, I know, but the remark stung me.

'What, to be run over by you? Try minding your own business!'

'I am an' all,' he bawled over his shoulder. 'What's the bleeding street for?'

'For turds like you!' I retorted.

'Bleeding dogs!' he screamed, almost falling off his bicycle in his rage and excitement as he swivelled his body round to hurl the denunciation at me.

'Arseholes!' I replied.

He made some further comment before he disappeared, wobbling into the mist, but I did not catch it. Nor could it have signified. There was no more to be said. I had had the last word.

It will be seen then that this is a subject which arouses strong passions in the human breast. And my accuser had authority on his side. It is an offence for dogs to foul the sidewalk. But only if they are on the lead and therefore (as it is quaintly phrased) under control. Multitudes of urban dogs roam the streets by them-selves, lifting their legs or tails upon the man-made world as necessity or fancy takes them, and can hardly be brought to court. The answer would seem to be: Don't put your dog on the lead.

I never had a moment's doubt in this matter myself. Having spent an anxious year at the beginning of my relationship with Tulip in persuading her that the side-walks were safer than the streets, and having fixed this prime rule of conduct firmly in her flighty head, I had no intention of confusing her with exceptions. The offi-cial notion seemed to be that one should train one's dog to squat in the gutter, but I did not need the cautionary tale told me by a sad young man in a public house to perceive the folly of that.

A model citizen, he had conscientiously taught his own animal this public-spirited practice. One day when, unobserved by him, for his attention was modestly averted, the dog was obediently crouching in the gutter of Tooting Broadway, a truck, drawing into the curb, ran over it and broke its back. That was six months ago, he said, gulping down his drink, but the creature's screams still haunted his sleep. Besides, I live and shop in the Lower Richmond Road, which with its concealing curves and flashing traffic is one of the most dangerous streets in Southwest London. Even upon the narrower stretches of its sidewalk one feels scarcely safe, for the vehicles whizz by within a foot or so of the curb. So I had already come to my own independent conclusion that the alternative to Tulip fouling the sidewalk was that she ran the risk of being killed, and that however strongly certain pedestrians and shopkeepers might hold the view that the latter would be preferable, she should never receive instructions from me to go into the street for any purpose whatever.

Nevertheless I have a considerate mind. I am able to see other people's points of view. I know that there are few things upon which it is a positive pleasure to tread. Whenever I take Tulip out, therefore, I always offer her opportunities to relieve herself in places relatively inoffensive to humanity before entering the busy streets of crowds and shops. To start with there is the Embankment, to which I have already referred. Although this is a carriageway, it is popularly used as a promenade by the people of Putney, who stroll up and down it by the river with their dogs, often on the street for the simple reason that its single footpath is discontinuous, interrupted for long stretches by boating ramps, and frequently submerged by the flooding tide. So little distinction, in fact, can be made between street and sidewalk that I consider none where Tulip is concerned. If she does not take immediate advantage of this, we dawdle on in the direction of Putney Bridge (we are generally making for a bus in the High Street) where another narrow ramp slants obliquely down into the mud of the foreshore. Here, amid the flotsam and jetsam of wood, cork, bottles, old tin cans, french letters, and the swollen bodies of drowned cats, dogs and birds left by the tide, she is often moved to open her bowels. If not, we pass on again (hurriedly now, for some fifty yards of sidewalk separate us from our next objective) to another species of refuse dump on the other side of the bridge, the ancient cemetery of Putney Church. The dead are less particular and more charitable than the living. It is a charming little cemetery; the few pretty nineteenth-century head-stones on the water side lean under acacia trees upon a grassy bank that slopes to a low river wall: swans float below. At the back of the church, where Hotpoint House now stands, lived 'that excellent woman, Mrs. Catherine Porten, the true mother of my mind as well as of my health,' as her nephew, Gibbon, who passed much of his youth in her house, described her. Strangely peaceful and secluded, although it lies just below the busy bridge, this small churchyard draws others, besides Tulip and myself, for their private purposes: upon the flattened grass beneath the tombstones in summertime I occasionally find coins, which, unnoticed in the darkness, have slipped out of trouser pockets, and other indications that the poor fleeting living, who have nowhere of their own, have been there to make love among the dead. To what better use could such a place be put? And are not its ghosts gladdened that so beautiful a young creature as Tulip should come here for her needs, whatever they may be? Here, springing from their long-forgotten bones, rankly grow her medicinal grasses, the coarse quitch grass which she searches out to pluck and eat when she wishes to make herself sick, and that other sort of grass she uses to bind and cleanse her bowels; and here too, I hope—it is our last chance—she will unburden herself beside the mortal remains of Caroline, Dowager Countess of Kingston (d. 1823) or of Mr. Stephen Robinson (d. 1827).

But the trouble with dogs is that they are not always inclined to relieve themselves when one desires them to do so, and we cannot hang about the cemetery for ever. Nor would the matter be settled if she did oblige me here. For dogs differ from people, who are usually able to get the business over and done with in one, by having a number of bowel actions during the course of a walk. The fact, therefore, that she may have left a lavish affair upon the Embankment is no sort of guarantee that she will not wish to leave another outside the doors of Woolworth's in the High Street ten minutes later, and then a third and a fourth at intervals thereafter. This truth, which is a general one, makes nonsense of all those official notices which request or command one to control one's dog in this respect. Indeed, I gaze wth incredulity at the folly displayed by local councils in the posters and enamelled signs they put up all over the place, regardless of expense. Putney is loaded with these signs, clamped to the stems of lamp posts or screwed into walls, especially the walls of alley ways. They read:

Wandsworth Borough Council. To dog owners. Please assist in maintaining PUBLIC HEALTH by restraining your dog from fouling footpaths. It is an offence to allow them to do so. the penalty being 40/−.

Overlooking the peculiar grammar and punctuation of this piece of literature, what does it mean? Here is an alley way stretching ahead of me for two or three hundred yards. It is enclosed by high walls. There is no escape from it except forwards or back. Dogs do not hold up their paws and say 'May I?' They simply squat and begin. What do I do if Tulip suddenly squats in the middle of it? How does one restrain a dog who has begun? Anxious as I am to assist in maintaining PUBLIC HEALTH, I should be interested to know what method the Town Clerk would have me employ. The weakness of his position is visible both in the notice itself, which starts with a request and ends with a threat, and in the fact that these alley ways are dotted with offences from end to end.

I remember seeing a young woman attempting to sat-isfy the requirements of the law. It was a moving spec-tacle. Her problem might seem simpler than the one I have set by placing Tulip in an alley; nevertheless she made a deplorable hash of it. The incident occurred at the north end of Sloane Street, and I observed it com-fortably from the top of a stationary bus. It was late in the morning, there were plenty of people about, and the lady was walking below me with her Poodle, which was on the lead. As they were passing a cleaners the dog was taken short. Quickly arranging his posterior against the wall of the shop, he began. With a sharp cry of dismay his mistress hauled him across the broad sidewalk to the gutter. It cannot be very pleasant to be dragged about by one's neck at such a moment; in any case the lady's interference could hardly have been more ill timed, and she was now convicted of earlier errors, she had been feeding her dog unwisely and too well. By the time he was safely in the gutter he had finished, and the sidewalk was impassable. If only she had left the good, intelligent creature to his own modest devices, all would have been, if not well, at any rate considerably better.

Tulip sometimes embarrasses me, too. She delivered herself once in front of a greengrocer's shop—and this on the way home from a long walk on Putney Common where she had already left as much as I supposed her to contain. But in the very entrance to the shop, whose stalls abutted on the sidewalk, she squatted again. I had made some purchases here in my time, and knew the grocer and his wife for a surly, disobliging couple.

37

Fortunately they were both busy inside the shop, which was otherwise deserted. Hoping, therefore, that they would not observe Tulip, and intending, by putting distance between us, to disown her if they did, I hastened by, hissing at her to 'Hurry up, for God's sake!' as I passed. Then a terrible thought struck me. If they did happen to notice her, might they not startle her out into the traffic by firing at her a potato or a sprout? I glanced back. Tulip had just finished and was following me; but at that very instant the man and his wife, perceiving the addition to their frontage, flew angrily out and caught my eye. Useless now to pretend ignorance, yet I continued on my way, affecting not to hear the accusations they hurled after me. Then my conscience smote me. This was cowardly and unchristian conduct. True they were horrid people, but no doubt they had their burdens like the rest of us, and Tulip's gift would not help to uplift their hearts to a sweeter view of life. It was rough on them, in short; and as soon as this noble thought occurred to me, I retraced my steps. The couple, who had now withdrawn into the interior, glowered at me over their barricades of vegetables.

'I'm sorry about my dog,' I said. 'It's difficult to prevent such things happening, but if you'll give me some newspaper or a bucket of water and a brush, I'll clear it up for you.'

Neither of them made any reply to this courteous speech, but the man silently handed me some pieces of paper. Unfortunately, this was one of those periods when the state of Tulip's bowels was disquieting me, and I had no cause now, when I had an extra reason for desiring a change, for any of that jubilation recorded by General Bertrand on April 12, 1821. It took me some time to swab it up, but I was thorough. When at last I straightened myself, only the sour-faced wife was visible in the shop. It was now her turn to pretend not to catch my eye.

'Well, that's done,' I said cheerfully. Without a word she turned her back on me. 'You could say "Thank you," ' I added mildly.

'Why should I?' she retorted, with a brief, contemptuous look.

Standing there with my hands full, I had an impulse to drop it all back on the pavement, but I restrained myself. Women are dangerous, especially women of the working class. It is always a mistake to ruffle them. They stop at nothing and they never let go. Like a *tricoteuse* of the French Revolution, this implacable lady would knit and gossip beside the guillotine as my head fell. But it was not for my own sake that I carried my good deed away. We passed here frequently upon our saunters, and I feared now that, to the greengrocer's wife, Tulip's death cries as, in dodging some vegetable missile, she went under a bus, would sound like music.

But as I have remarked, Tulip's intestines have a debit as well as a credit side, and while the latter is sometimes a vexation to others, the former can be a serious inconvenience to me. I am taking her away for a country visit, for example, and since we have a train to catch and a journey ahead of us it is imperative that she should get her business over before we start. But on such occasions attention to her natural needs seems as absent from her thought as it is urgently present in mine. Discomposed, perhaps, by the signs of something unusual afoot (she is perturbed by the sight of packing and will often unpack my things as fast as I put them in, even though I assure her that she is coming too), she fails to connect the Embankment, the ramp, or the churchyard with the ideas they normally suggest. Never mind, we still have the walk over the bridge to the railway station; no doubt the exercise will stimulate her. Not at all. We reach the station yard, but Tulip has still failed in her duty.

'Come on, Tulip,' I say, 'get you does done, there's a good girl.'

She casts at me a jolly look but nothing more. A Victoria train rumbles over the railway bridge above our heads and draws into the station. I have left ample time for our connection, but we could have had this train if Tulip had cooperated. Far from that, however, she is now regarding me with the most irritating expectancy, as though it were me, not her, of whom something was required. There is nothing for it but to walk her round the station, and hitching my heavy rucksack more firmly onto my shoulders, we make the longish circuit. Tulip bounds blithely ahead.

'Come on, Tulip, be a sport. Shitsy-witsy, you know.'

If she knows she gives no sign. I observe in the roadway a magnificent specimen of the very thing I want and draw her attention to it. She piddles on it. Now we are back at the station yard. Another train rumbles overhead. I begin to get anxious and therefore cross.

'Tulip! Pull yourself together!'

She puts on her frog face. That is to say she compresses her jaws so that her face looks rather flat and her lips pout out all round. I know this face well. It is her teasing one and means she is going to provoke me. Usually it amuses me. It does not amuse me now.

'Don't be tiresome, Tulip! I'll give you a bang!'

She barks at me, retreating a little; then seizes me playfully by the foot. There is nothing for it but to circumambulate the station again, and resignedly I hitch my load higher up my back. Round the station we go, Tulip staring at me as though I have taken leave of my senses. I glance at my watch. Time is passing if nothing else. I call her to me and massage her, her back, her stomach, squeeze her indeed. She enjoys this and becomes flirtatious. Maddening dog! Whatever possessed me to possess her! It will be a miracle now if we catch our train. Worn out before the journey has begun, I sit down on a wall at last and stare moodily at her . . .

But I fear I may be presenting her in an inconsiderate, even insensitive, light, and that will not do. She too has her feelings, and now that I have put the human point of view it is proper to attend to hers, and to make, also, a few brief observations on what are commonly regarded as the insanitary habits of dogs, whose manners, on the whole, seem to me admirable.

Like many other animals, adult dogs have an instinct for what may be called a comfortable and cleanly modesty over the particular bodily function I have been discussing, and some of my country friends tell me that their dogs evince a scrupulosity as strict as our own in their desire to perform it in seclusion. But to a town dog the outside world is too difficult a problem. Opportunities for privacy are rare, and though Tulip may often be seen to take advantage of them when they appear to offer, as when she turns through an open gate into someone's front garden, peace and quiet are seldom the reward she reaps. Whatever choice for modesty she makes, in short, is pretty sure to be wrong; she even earned a rebuke once for using a public lavatory, and not on the grounds that it was a Gentlemen's. She had followed me down into it, and was taking no greater advantage of the place than to micturate a little in the stall beside my own, when the attendant rushed out and shooed her away.

'I've got to bucket that over now!' he complained bitterly. 'They're not allowed down 'ere, gov.'

It is scarcely to be wondered at, therefore, that in the course of years her sensibilities should have become blunted. But she has them still, and they are more easily perceived indoors.

I have no grounds or garden into which she may retire and conceal herself behind a rhododendron bush. All I can offer her is an open-air terace, and this, she knows, is at her disposal for any purpose whatever. But perhaps because she also knows that I sometimes sit on it myself, she only uses it for the major function when she cannot wait. And then she always comes to tell me. I may be shaving in the bathroom, when Tulip will suddenly arrive with the air of one who has grave tidings to impart, and move around me in a bashful manner, trying to catch my eye. I know at once what her news is and allow myself to be led out to inspect it. Then I get a pail of water and sluice it away, while she looks on with manifest satisfaction.

If canine faeces are objectionable to the human race,

they are rejected by dogs as well. This may seem an overstatement to those people who observe, with pained disapproval, the ways dogs greet each other in the street, and put upon such behavior a perverse and unhygienic construction. But what the animals are investigating here is that secretion of the anal glands to which I have already referred, the scent of which provides them with information.* Whatever perversity there may be in this matter is exhibited by people themselves when, in their endeavor to impose their own standards of conduct upon their dogs, they prevent them from smelling one another's bottoms.

Dogs read the world through their noses and write their history in urine. Urine is another and highly complex source of social information; it is a language, a code, by means of which they not only express their feelings and emotions, but communicate with and appraise each other. Tulip is particularly instructive in this matter when she is in season, for on these occasions she has numerous callers who leave the marks of their attention round the front door. On her way in and out she reads, with her long black nose, these superimposed stains, and

---

* Tulip, whom I brush and comb daily to rid her of her loose hairs, seems to me generally quite odorless. But occasionally the scent of her anal glands is strongly evident. It is a musky smell which I myself do not find disagreeable. Can it be to this that W. H. Hudson was referring when he wrote, in *A Hind in Richmond Park*, that all dogs, even the most 'petted lapdog, fed delicately and washed and brushed regularly every day,' smelt to him like carrion, 'not the smell of carrion lying and drying in the sun, but of a dead animal lying and decomposing in a pool of water in hot weather'? This curious passage, so thorough in its nastiness, has always puzzled me.

the care with which she studies them is so meticulous
that she gives the impression of actually identifying her
acquaintances and friends.

She has two kinds of urination, Necessity and Social.
Different stances are usually, though not invariably,
adopted for each. In necessity she squats squarely and
abruptly, right down on her shins, her hind legs forming
a kind of dam against the stream that gushes out from
behind; her tail curves up like a scimitar; her expression is complacent. For social urination, which is mostly
preceded by the act of smelling, she seldom squats, but
balances herself on one hind leg, the other being withdrawn or cocked up in the air. The reason for this seems
obvious; she is watering some special thing and wishes
to avoid touching it. It may also be that in this attitude
she can more accurately bestow her drops. Often they
are merely drops, a single token drop will do, for the
social flow is less copious. The expression on her face is
business-like, as though she were signing a check.

She attends socially to a wide range of objects. The
commonest group are the droppings, both liquid and
solid, of other animals. Fresh horse dung has a special
attraction for her and is always liberally sprayed. Then
she sprinkles any food that has been thrown about—
buns, bones, fish, bread, vomit—unless it is food she
wishes to eat. Dead and decaying animals are carefully
attended to. There are advanced stages of decay, when
flesh turns into a kind of tallow, which affect her so
deeply that urination appears to be an inadequate expression of her feelings. Try as she may she cannot lift
her leg, and tottering round the object in a swooning way
would prostrate herself upon it if the meddling voice of
authority did not intervene. One day there was a human

corpse, which had been fished out of the river, lying under a tarpaulin by the water's edge awaiting an ambulance to take it away, and Tulip approached it with that air of shrinking curiosity that dogs often evince towards large, draped, motionless objects in the road, such as sacks or bundles. She had never seen a human corpse before, and I should have been interested to observe how she behaved to it, but there were other spectators standing by and I thought it wiser to call her off. Human beings are so arrogant. They think nothing of chopping off the head of some dead animal, a calf or a pig, twisting its features into a ludicrous grimace, so that it appears to be grinning, winking, or licking its cold lips, and displaying it in a shop window as a comic advertisement of its own flesh. But any supposed indignity to *their* dead would be a very different matter, though whatever statement Tulip had made on this occasion would at any rate have had the merit of being serious.

She drips also upon drains, disinfectants and detergents (in a street of doorsteps it is generally the one most recently scoured that she selects), and pieces of newspaper. Once she spared a few drops for a heap of socks and shoes left on the foreshore of the river by some rowing men who had gone sculling. Following her antics with the utmost curiosity, I used to wonder what on earth she was up to. I saw that, excepting perhaps for the newspapers, unless something savory had been wrapped up in them or she was moved by printers' ink, all these objects had a quality in common, smell; even so, why did she pee on them? It could not be because other dogs had done so before her, for that only pushed the question further back: who began, and why? Nor did I think she was staking a personal claim; nothing in her subsequent behavior suggested appropriation. I came to the conclusion that she was simply expressing an appreciative interest; she was endorsing these delectable things with her signature, much as we underline a book we are reading.

Tulip has no scruple about wetting herself with her urine, and does so every morning when she visits my terrace: an event, incidentally, which she never troubles to report. If I wish to inform myself about it I can easily do so by feeling her hind legs, a piece of intimacy which she perfectly understands and which always amuses us both. Nor does she seem to mind other dogs wetting her, for it happens that, when she is easing herself on the Embankment below, some local dog, excited perhaps by the fresh scent of her glandular discharge, may lift his leg over her rump as she squats. But as I have already shown, she takes elaborate care not to soil herself with her faeces, and displays a similar distaste for those of other adult dogs. Though she may venture an extremely cautious inquiring sniff at such things that lie in her path, she will then give them a markedly wide and disdainful berth; if she should happen to tread in one by accident, she flickers her foot and limps as though she had gone lame.

But her sensitivity can be more vividly illustrated if, Tulip permitting, I continue the journey we were attempting to make a short while ago and recount our experiences when we first went country visiting. Very few of my country friends ask her to stay with them; they mostly go in for cats who go out for Tulip; those who have no pets of their own are a little forgetful about inviting her twice; her unconquerable belief that every building we enter, even a railway carriage, belongs from that moment exclusively to us, may have something to do with it; people seem to resent being challenged whenever they approach their own sitting or dining rooms.

Our first host was a Captain Pugh, who had served with me in France in the 1914 war. I had seen nothing of him for a great many years, then he suddenly turned up again as people do and asked me down to stay. He was farming in Kent. How can an urban dog owner go into the country without his dog? I said I should be delighted to come if I could bring Tulip. It appeared, however, that Mrs. Pugh, of whom, until then, I had never heard, kept Cairns, and although I assured Pugh that Tulip was very partial to little dogs, negotiations were suspended. Then Mrs. Pugh went off with her Cairns for a night elsewhere, my invitation was renewed to include Tulip, and she and I travelled down into Kent together.

Actually I remembered very little about my host, except that he had been an officer who had managed to combine great courage and efficiency with a marked indolence of habit. Whenever, for instance, he had wanted his servant or his orderly, as he frequently did, it had been his custom to fire his revolver into the wall of his dugout—one shot for the servant, two for the orderly—to save himself the exertion of shouting. An odd figure, and, as I was to discover, set in his ways; his whims were, indeed, to contribute to the misfortunes that befell us beneath his roof.

He emerged from a cowshed as we entered his extensive domain, and guided us up to the house. Poultry came into view, pecking about on either side of the long drive, and Pugh interrupted his conversation about old times to remark briefly that he hoped Tulip would not 'go after' them as they were laying rather well at present. I hoped not too; but she had met hens only once before, so I had no means of telling whether she would recall the smacking she had received on that occasion. I could have put her on the lead, I suppose, and that may have been what Pugh was hinting at; but how can one gauge the intelligence of one's animal if one never affords it the chance to display any? And, to my astonishment and pride, only one sharp cautionary word was needed, when I saw her tail go up and a wolfish gleam enter her eye, to remind her of her lesson: the poultry were passed unscathed. Indeed, we should have gained Pugh's residence in faultless style, had it not been for a ginger cat that was idling in the shrubbery. I was quite unprepared for this cat, which had never been mentioned in the kind of farmyard inventory to which, in our correspondence about the Cairns, Pugh had apparently thought it advisable to extend his concern, so I was too late to prevent Tulip, who saw it first, from sailing into combat. She pursued it into a small potting shed that stood alongside the house. I apologized profusely; but it turned out to be not at all an important cat; it belonged to the category neither of pet nor of livestock, but was a mere hireling, engaged for the purpose of keeping down the mice, in which capacity, I gathered, it was not giving the utmost satisfaction; and since Pugh observed its narrow escape without apparent emotion, remarking offhandedly, as he clapped-to the potting-shed door, 'It can stay there now,' I permitted myself to be amused. Little did I think that this cat, who was scowling wrathfully at us through the dusty panes, was to take its revenge upon us later.

As I have said, Pugh's personal idiosyncrasies had gained ground. I scarcely saw him during my stay. He had arrived at the conclusion, which I might have foreseen if I had given the matter thought, that rest and relaxation were the key to efficient health, the art of life, so that the only problem that appeared to trouble him was whether, for half an hour or more, both before and after every meal, it should be 'Head-down' or 'Bed-down,' by which he meant whether it would be more rewording to nap on a sofa or to undress and return to bed. Earnestly recommending me to follow an example which, he declared, would enable me to derive the maximum amount of benefit from my short stay with him, his phrase was 'One rises like a giant refreshed'; and, indeed, that did seem to be the effect upon himself, for at those rare moments when he was not horizontal he would stalk about the farm buildings with great vigor, making many pertinent remarks in his military voice and spreading consternation among the cows. The house, which he had built himself, managed to be bleak without being actually cold; the wide wooden staircase, with its low treads to reduce leg-strain, was uncarpeted and so was the gallery above, on to which the bedroom doors opened. I had been allotted the bedroom of the absent Mrs. Pugh, a large room, strewn with a number of small mats and rugs, which adjoined the Captain's and communicated with it. Besides the bed, it contained, I was glad though not surprised to find, a comfortable sofa for Tulip: there was a sofa in every room, including the dining room and bathroom.

When Pugh finally retired, at an early hour, he observed that he was a light sleeper and therefore hoped that Tulip was a sound one. He added that he always slept with his passage door and window wide open in order to obtain the maximum amount of fresh air. In fact Tulip is a very quiet sleeper, though she will usually pay me one visit in the night and put her nose against my face. Perhaps I cry out in my dreams—or do not, and she wishes to reassure herself that I am not dead. It was, therefore, well precedented when she wakened me at about 2 A.M. on this particular night. I patted her drowsily and recomposed myself for slumber. But Tulip did not go away. Instead she rose up on her hind legs and pulled in an urgent kind of way, with her paw, at the shoulder I had turned towards her. Looking up, I could discern in the gloom the shape of her head with its tall ears cocked down at me as she stared intently into my face. What could she want? I fumbled about on the side-table for my matches and lighted the candle (the farm was too remote for electricity), whereupon Tulip hurried over to the door and stood in front of it, looking eagerly back at me.

'What's up, old girl?' I asked uneasily.

She made a little whinnying sound, pawed excitedly at the door and again turned her brilliant gaze upon me. Hell! I thought, can she possibly want to pee or something? She scarcely ever needed to relieve herself at night; she had done her duties often throughout the day, and (I looked at my watch) it was only four hours since I had taken her for a final tour of the grounds before Pugh locked and bolted his front door. Could she really want to go again? Not that in other circumstances I would have hesitated to take or let her out; but how in the world was I to get her past my host's open door at the head of the staircase and down the slithery wooden stairs which, I had already noticed, rang like a sounding-board beneath her tapping claws, without waking him? Even then, and all by the light of a candle, there was that heavy oak door at the bottom to be noiselessly un-locked and unbolted. . . .

'Tulip dear,' I said to the earnest face, 'you don't honestly want to, do you?'

Then her knell, and mine, sounded. The cat, still imprisoned in the potting-shed in the garden outside, yowled, and Tulip's bright eyes shifted to the window. So that was it! On all our numerous excursions round the grounds, during Pugh's bouts of 'Head-down' or 'Bed-down,' she had made a bee-line for this shed and taunted the cat, who had consolidated an already im-pregnable position by entrenching itself among some flower-pots on an upper shelf. Doubtless its maledictions had been provoking her while I slept. I extinguished the candle and settled back on my pillow. But Tulip was in-stantly beside me, clawing at my face and arm.

'Don't be tiresome, Tulip! Go back to bed! We'll visit the cat in the morning.'

She left me then, but she did not go to her sofa. She returned to the door, snuffled at the bottom of it, and then subsided heavily against it with a sigh. But almost at once she was up again and prowling about the dark room. Silence. Then I heard plop-plop-plop. I fumbled for my matches now with such haste that I knocked over several objects on my table with a loud clatter. When the candle was lit, Tulip was coming towards me from the other side of the room. Wagging her tail and gazing at me with soft, glowing eyes, she kissed my cheek. And, indeed, she couldn't have helped it. I saw that at once when I got out of bed to look. She couldn't have retained it for a moment longer. But—I was deeply touched—she had selected her place with as much care as the lay-out of the room allowed. Avoiding all the rugs, she had laid her mess on the linoleum and as far from me as she could get, against Pugh's communicating door.

I was more than touched. I was dreadfully upset. My pretty animal, my friend, who reposed in me a loving confidence that was absolute, had spoken to me as plainly as she could. She had used every device that lay in her poor brute's power to tell me something, and I had not understood. True I had considered her meaning, but she was not to know that for I had rejected it; nor could I ever explain to her that I had not totally misunderstood but only doubted: to her it must have seemed that she had been unable to reach me after all. How wonderful to have had an animal come to one to communicate where no communication is, over the incommunicability of no common speech, to ask a personal favor! How wretched to have failed! Alas for the gulf that separates man and beast: I had had my chance; now it was too late to bridge it. Oh yes, I could throw my arms about her as I did, fondle and praise her in my efforts to reassure her that it was all my fault and she was the cleverest person in the world. But what could she make of that? I had failed to take her meaning, and nothing I could ever do could put that right.

She lay now on her sofa watching me swab it up. For that had to be done at once. What did she think as she observed me take all the trouble which, one might say, she had tried so hard to avert? For it needed a good twenty minutes to clear the mess up, and numerous visits to the W.C. half-way down the stairs, with the paper linings of Mrs. Pugh's chest-of-drawers. Poor Pugh! It was not, I fear, with the look of a giant refreshed that he appeared at the breakfast table later. He said kindly that it was of no consequence. But it was. Tulip was never asked again.

Did she lose some confidence in me at that moment? I have often sadly wondered. But I cannot be sure. For the next time we went visiting I was rather unwell and took a drug to make me sleep. I shall never know, therefore, whether she tried to wake me or not. Her problem this time was both easier and more difficult. It was a far grander house than Captain Pugh's, with a lot of unoccupied bedrooms, one of which communicated with mine. Since the communicating door on this occasion was ajar, Tulip's main strategic problem of removing herself from my presence was solved; she had only to push the door open and go into the next room. On the other hand, the house was carpeted throughout with handsome Indian carpeting. There was not an inch of linoleum or skirting-board anywhere. It so happened, however, that in this large adjoining room there was a solitary rug, small, cheap and suitably brown, spread upon the pile carpet in front of a dressing table, and Tulip selected this for her purpose. (*Did* she try to wake me first? Or did she say to herself, 'Alas, he wouldn't understand'? How I wish I knew!) At any rate, she made this delicate choice for cleanliness, unobtrusiveness and protective coloring, and thereby defeated her own ends. For the housemaid who brought up my breakfast the following morning and had already learnt to approach any place where Tulip lay with circumspection, thoughtfully decided not to enter our room at all. Instead, she carried my breakfast into the adjoining one by its passage door and, quietly crossing it, placed the tray upon the dressing table. She then retraced her steps and, coming round to my own passage door, tapped upon it to tell me what she had done. What she had done was only perceived later in the day, and then a bottle of ammonia and several hours' hard work were required before the poor girl's retraced steps across the white carpet were wholly obliterated.

After the episode of the greengrocer's wife, it is a pleasure to record that at this time sympathy and moral support came from the least expected quarter. I was in need of both, for Tulip and I had been invited to the house for several days. Now that she had improvised a W.C. for herself, would she not return to it every night? And what could I do to circumvent this? Should I, for instance, strew sheets of brown paper in front of the dressing table where the rug had been? But the housemaid, upon whom the brunt of the business had fallen, assured me that it was quite unnecessary to take precautions of any kind. This good-natured girl, it transpired, had had much to do with dogs in her time, and she stoutly maintained that Tulip would not repeat the offence, that the only reason why she had committed it at all was that dogs are highly nervous and excitable creatures, and that travel, when they are unused to it, often upsets their digestions. Her diagnosis and prediction were perfectly correct. Tulip never did it again.

The story has an even happier ending. If I did forfeit any of Tulip's confidence at this period, I have reason to believe that I recovered it later. For the events I have related took place many years ago when she was young and a shade irresponsible, and our love was new. There came a day, however, when we were walking in Wimbledon woods and she suddenly added my urine, which I had been obliged to void, to the other privileged objects of her social attention. How touched I was! How honored I felt! 'Oh, Tulip! Thank you,' I said.

And now she always does it. No matter how preoccupied her mind may be with other things, such as rabbiting, she will always turn back, before following me, to the place where she saw me relieve myself—for nothing that I do escapes her—to sprinkle her own drops upon mine. So I feel that if ever there were differences between us they are washed out now. I feel a proper dog.

3 · Trial and Error

Soon after Tulip came into my possession I set about finding a husband for her. She had had a lonely and frustrated life hitherto; now she should have a full one. A full life naturally included the pleasures of sex and maternity, and although I could not, of course, accom-

modate a litter of puppies in my small flat, that was a
matter to which I would give my attention later.

The prospect of mating her presented no other serious
problem. Slender though my knowledge was, it seemed
sufficient. Bitches came into season or, more vulgarly,
heat twice a year. The heat lasted for three weeks. During the first week the vagina gradually opened; during
the third it gradually closed. Mating was accomplished
at the peak, in the second week. It was all plain sailing.
Indeed, such difficulty as I envisaged lay in the opposite direction, in preventing her from being mated—in
protecting her, that is to say, from the attention of undesirable suitors. Undesirable suitors were stray dogs of
other breeds, or of no breed at all; for although I had
no profit-making interest in the matter, so beautiful a
creature as Tulip should certainly have children as
pretty as herself. The only question that remained to
be settled therefore was the choice of a suitable mate—
the question, in fact, that confronts us all, but simplified
in the case of bitches by the availability of a stud system
of dogs for the hiring. Partly out of thrift, however, I
discarded this solution. Why pay a fee for hiring a husband when there were quantities of good-looking Alsatians about who might be borrowed for nothing if one
got to know their owners? But how did one get to know
their owners? Tulip's next heat—the third of her life,
but the first since she entered mine—was close at hand.
I could not rely upon a chance encounter. Might not a
vet help? Any vet would probably include an Alsatian
or two among his patients; it would be easy for him to
sound the owners and put me in touch. All this a local
vet obligingly did. He provided me with the address of a
Mr. Blandish who lived in Sheen and owned a good

Alsatian named Max whom he was willing to lend. Vets at this early period of my life in the dog world seemed to me an impatient race, but I trespassed further upon this one's time to inquire whether there were any particularly favorable days in the second week for putting the two animals together. That, said he, was a question the bitch herself would decide, but the ninth to eleventh days were considered normal. He added that I should find out whether Max had had any previous sexual history. Why? I asked. With a weary smile the vet replied that mating dogs was not always so simple a matter as I seemed to suppose, and that since Tulip was inexperienced it would be helpful to have a sire who knew the ropes. He then turned his back on me.

The house was large, solid and detached, and that it was probably the right one was indicated, as I pressed the bell, by a short rumble of gruff barks within. Max was then revealed as a heavy, handsome dog with the grave deportment of the old family retainer. His stolid figure silently barred my entry, until a quiet word from his master authorized him to admit me. When I was invited into the sitting-room he followed after and, assuming a dignified posture on the hearth-rug, kept me under close surveillance: the house and its management clearly belonged to him. To have offered him any kind of familiarity, it was plain, would have been as shocking a breach of eitquette as if one had attempted to stroke the butler.

Mr. Blandish, who was hearty, prosperous, middle-aged and bald, seated himself beside me on the sofa and gave me a cigarette.

'Matches! Matches!' he then exclaimed, in a petulant voice. 'Are there no matches in the house!'

Considerably startled by this outburst, I said soothingly: 'Oh, never mind. I think I've got some.'

But before I could begin to fumble, Max had lumbered to his feet and, with a swaying motion of the hips, crossed the room. Picking up an outsize box that was lying on a stool, he brought it to his master. Mr. Blandish accepted it without comment and lighted our cigarettes, while Max stood obsequiously at his elbow.

'Thank you, Max,' he then said, in a negligent manner, and handed the box back to the dog, who replaced it on the stool and gravely resumed his watchful position on the rug.

This unnerving incident was not permitted to interrupt the Blandishes' flow of polite conversation. They plied me with questions about Tulip and expressed their delight at the projected alliance. They had had Max for six years and had always wished for an opportunity of this kind; his happiness was their only concern in the transaction. These remarks gave me the opening I needed to put the question the vet had advised me to put, but the alarming exhibition of canine sagacity I had just witnessed had so shaken me that I hardly knew how to frame the inquiry in Max's presence. Avoiding his eye, I stammered:

'Then will this be his first experience of—with the opposite sex? The vet seemed to think there might be difficulties unless—'

But Mr. Blandish displayed no sense of delicacy.

'Oh, you needn't worry about that!' said he, with a guffaw. 'Max knows his oats all right!'

59

I coughed.

'He's been married before, then?'

'He's never been churched, it's true,' said Mr. Blandish, 'but when we were down in the country a couple of years ago, he happened upon a stray bitch in heat—not at all a classy one, either—and had his wicked way with her on the spot. He'll be delighted to repeat the performance with Tulip, I can assure you!' he added gleefully.

'Oh, then that's all right. It was only that, Tulip being a virgin, the vet thought—'

'Leave it all to me,' said Mr. Blandish gaily. 'I've got a very reliable little book—not that Max will need to look anything up in it!'

I was then invited to bring Tulip along for a formal introduction to her betrothed. When I got up to go, Max preceded me into the hall and, interposing his bulk between myself and my hat, required another permissive word from his master before I was able to pick it up, in case, Mr. Blandish explained, I took the wrong one.

The formal introduction was effected a few days later, and if Tulip failed to make a bad impression on the Blandishes, it was not, I thought, for any want of trying. Of the kind of impression she made on Max there seemed to me no doubt at all. The sound of his throaty rumble as we advanced up the drive announced that he was on duty, and the opening door disclosed him, planted squarely on the threshold as before, his master's hand upon his collar. The affianced pair gingerly sniffed each other's noses, and Max's tail rose righer in the air and began to wave majestically from side to side: he was

clearly preparing to do the canine honors. Much grati-
fied by this exhibition of tender feeling, Mr. Blandish
bade us enter, and both animals were released in the
hall. But no sooner had Max approached Tulip, in the
most affable manner, to extend his acquaintance with
her, than she rounded vigorously upon him and drove
him down the passage into what appeared to be the pantry with his tail between his legs. From then on, it seemed
to me, she behaved abominably. She investigated all
round the Blandishes' sitting-room in a thorough, dubious and insulting way, as though she could scarcely believe her nose, and then refused to sit or lie down, but
constantly interrupted our conversation by nattering at
me to take her away, staring at me imperiously with her
exclamatory face. When I pretended not to notice her,
she tried to pull me out of my chair by her own lead,
which I always carried clipped round my neck. To the
Blandishes and their overtures of friendship she paid
not the slightest heed; they might, indeed, not have been
present; and whenever Max was emboldened to emerge
from the pantry to join us, she instantly chased him back
into it again.

I apologised for her behavior, but I need not have done
so. The Blandishes had taken no offence. On the contrary, they were positively enchanted by her beauty and
the femininity, as they termed it, of her conduct; and
every time she drove poor Max out of his own sitting-
room, Mr. Blandish was, indeed, so excessively amused,
remarking with a chuckle that she was a sweet and
proper little bitch and that he could see they would get
along famously together when her time came, that I
could not help wondering from what source of knowl-

edge such optimism derived and found my gaze dwelling speculatively upon Mrs. Blandish, who was a pretty little woman considerably younger than her husband.

Tulip's time would come, said he, between her seventh and ninth day. The nuptials, he added jovially, would take place in his back garden. I ventured to remark that my own information was that a later day in the second week might be better, but he replied firmly that I was mistaken, his reliable little book recommended the seventh to the ninth days and I could safely leave matters to his judgment. His assertiveness overbore me, but I was dissatisfied nevertheless. Ignorant though I was, it seemed to me a pity that the two animals should have no opportunity to get better acquainted before the moment arrived, and I therefore suggested diffidently, that, since we were neighbors, they might be exercised together occasionally between now and the event.

'What a good idea!' cried Mrs. Blandish. But her husband was instantly and flatly opposed. It was Mrs. Blandish, he observed drily, who took Max for his walks while he himself was at work, and he could not permit her to have any part in this business, at any rate in his absence. When we left, Max was again withdrawn from hiding to say goodbye to Tulip, but he could not be induced to approach her closely. This restored Mr. Blandish to his previous good humor.

'His other wife bit him in the shoulder,' he chortled, rubbing his hands; 'but he won't at all mind a few more bites when his time with Tulip comes!' He said this with such gusto that I glanced again involuntarily at Mrs. Blandish, who was smiling roguishly at him with her small, even teeth.

. . .

Dear Tulip maintained, with diabolical consistency, the perverseness she had hitherto shown: she chose (cleverly, some might think) to come in to heat in the midst of the most arctic winter this chilly country had suffered for fifty years. But it was my first experience of her in this condition and I was enchanted. That small dark bud, her vulva, became gradually swollen and more noticeable amid the light gray fur of her thighs as she walked ahead of me, and sometimes it would set up, I supposed, a tickle or a trickle or some other sensation, for she would suddenly squat down in the road and fall to licking it. At such moments I could see how much larger it had grown and the pretty pink of its lining. Then there were spots of blood on her silvery shins. She did not bleed much, nor did she smell; I should not have minded either. I was touched by the mysterious process at work within her and felt very sweet towards her.

She also felt very sweet towards me. She was always coming to me as I sat reading or writing, and would push her rump up against by knee, gazing at me over her shoulder with an intent look I learnt to know well. She would stay there for a long time, motionless, looking earnestly up at me, until I put down a hand to stroke her head and back, or (which she greatly preferred) her stomach with its little button nipples. Then, as soon as I stopped, she would mount my leg, standing up like a kangaroo to clasp me round the thigh and try to work herself against me. I would gently deter her from these practices, from which, it seemed to me, she could derive nothing but physical harm, and she would often then go out into the passage and, reaching up to the coat rack, clasp my old tweed overcoat in her arms instead. I had to deter her from this also, for she kept catching the upper claws of her front legs in the stuff of the coat, and this hurt her and caused her to cry out.

It was scarcely to be expected that Mr. Blandish would relish being reminded of his engagement, for the country had lain under snow for many days. He complained that, and sounded as if, he had a heavy cold, but he kept his word and appointed an afternoon in the following week, Tulip's eighth or ninth day: since I was too inexperienced to know precisely when one started to count, whether at the first faint smear of blood or when the discharge became more copious, I was uncertain which. The day dawned colder, if possible, than any that had preceded it, and it was in no very cheerful frame of mind that I deserted my fireside and set out with her across Putney Common. Tulip, however, was in an ecstasy of joy; this was the first snow she had ever seen and, warmly clad in her fine sable-gray coat, she flew about in it with childish glee. She was still bleeding a little, and my most recent piece of lore on the subject was that dogs would not copulate with bitches until the flow of blood had ceased. Be that as it may, we were accompanied as usual by a small escort of ardent admirers. They did not trouble me much, however, partly because they all looked too small to be a serious menace, partly because she herself was so obedient. And eventually she lost many of them for me by delaying tactics worthy of Hippomenes—if that was her intention and she was not, on the contrary, a bungling Ariadne with a too brittle thread. I had already noticed that her urine, in her present condition, appeared to provide her wooers with a most gratifying cordial, for they avidly lapped it up whenever she condescended to void it, which she frequently did. So heady was its effect that their jaws would at once start to drip and chatter together, not merely visibly but audibly. Now, squatting here and there upon other dogs' droppings or whatever odor attracted her, like some famous chef adding to a prepared dish the final exquisite flavor, the crowning touch, she left behind her in the snow as she flew a series of sorbets, and her crazed attendants were so often and so long delayed in licking them up that they eventually fell far behind.

Though his heavy cold persisted, Mr. Blandish received us amiably. I told him that Tulip was still bleeding, but he said that did not matter, he had his reliable little book and we would now see a marked change in Max's demeanor. This was perfectly true. The moment Tulip's scent reached him, he quickly discarded his servile role and was seen to be capable of manly emotions. Unhappily there was no corresponding change on Tulip's side. Never mind, said Mr. Blandish cheerfully, picking up the umbrella stand which had been overturned by Max in his headlong flight, everything would be quite all right when the two animals were left alone together in the garden, they would soon 'get down to business' then. But to be left alone together in the garden, it could not have been more evident, was the last thing that either of the two animals wished; Tulip's single purpose was not to be separated from me, while Max needed peremptory orders to withdraw him from the servants' quarters. Eventually, however, both of them were pushed out of the back door, at which Tulip barked and rattled until I commanded her to stop. Silence then fell, while Mr. Blandish and I gazed hopefully out of the kitchen window into the bleak and snow-patched garden. It was all the view we had, for the two dogs were nowhere to be seen—until Tulip's face with its pricked ears rose suddenly up to confront me accusingly through the glass.

I then told Mr. Blandish that if she was to pay any attention at all to Max I felt convinced she would have none to spare while so much of it was focused anxiously upon myself, and that I had better set her mind at rest by joining her outside. I added politely that, in view of his seedy condition, it would be unwise of him to take the risk of coming too.

'No, dear, you really shouldn't!' chimed in Mrs. Blandish, who had just come in. 'Let *me* go out with Mr. Ackerley.'

No speech could have been more considerate or more unwise.

'Nonsense!' said Mr. Blandish. 'I cannot allow you to venture out. I shall be quite all right,' and struggling into a thick overcoat and a pair of galoshes he accompanied me into the garden, where Tulip cast herself into my arms with an ardor I could have wished to see directed elsewhere. Max at first could not be found; he was eventually located skulking under the laurels at the front of the house.

The end of this fiasco will already be apparent. I do not remember how long we stood stamping our feet in that icy garden exhorting the two dogs, when they were momentarily together, to sexual intercourse, nor how many times Max was propelled from and stampeded back into the house. Tulip, whose fixed determination clearly was that he should approach neither me nor her, enjoyed herself hugely. Considering that Max was almost twice her size and weight, his conduct seemed to me craven.

At length Mr. Blandish, who had omitted to bring his

hat, began to feel a chill on his bald head and said he must have a covering. I offered to fetch it for him, but he said no, Max would bring it, it was one of his household duties. He spoke with pride; it was obviously another of Max's 'turns.' He therefore shouted up to Mrs. Blandish to send out his cap, and with it, Max, like a well-trained servant, albeit warily, soon emerged from the French windows.

'Thank you, Max,' said Mr. Blandish, extending a casual hand. But Tulip was having no nonsense of that sort. First by one barely distinct garden path, then by another, did Max (who had been taught not to walk on the beds) endeavor to carry out his master's wishes, which soon turned into vexed commands; but he was headed off and driven back over and over again, until, totally demoralized, he dropped the cap in the snow and slunk off for good, his proud mission unfulfilled.

This marked the end of Mr. Blandish's indulgence and our visit. I diffidently suggested that it might be worth while seeing whether the animals got on any better together when Tulip's heat was further advanced, but he replied, rather stuffily, that he feared he had no time to arrange it. On that we took our leave. 'You bad girl!' I said to Tulip as we trudged away through the snow; but she was now, when she had me back to herself, in her most disarming mood, and as soon as we were home she attempted to bestow upon my leg and my overcoat all the love that the pusillanimous Max had been denied.

My vet could help no further. Tulip's receptive period, he agreed, would continue for some days, but he had no more Alsatians on his books. He observed, tire-somely, that he had told me that mating dogs was not always a simple matter, and added, even more tire-somely, the belated information that when they were inexperienced it was often necessary to hold the bitch's head and guide the dog into position: the application of a little vaseline to the bitch sometimes helped to ex-cite and define the interest besides acting as a lubricant. But I am not easily deterred. I had seen a number of Alsatians on Putney Heath at various times, and I went in search of one now. I drew a blank. But the following day fortune favored me. A solitary gentleman with his dog was visible in the distance. I hastened after him and caught him up. It is even easier to talk to people about their dogs than about their children, and in this case the animal himself provided the introduction by coming up to be petted.

'Nice dog,' I said, thinking what a poor specimen he looked. 'What's his name?'

'Chum,' said his owner gloomily.

'He's friendly for an Alsatian.'

'That's just it! He goes up to anyone, and often goes off with them too. Other dogs as well. Sometimes I have quite a job to get him back, he's grown so disobedient. I don't know what's come over him. He was more of a pal once . . .'

'Has he a pedigree?' I asked politely, examining Chum with increasing dismay. Was he really good enough for Tulip? His ears managed to stand up, but he had scarcely any ruff and a pale, lean body like a greyhound.

'Oh yes, I paid quite a bit for him. I specially wanted an Alsatian, they're said to be so devoted.'

'How long have you had him?'

'Getting on for three years. And he's well looked after. I take a lot of trouble to please him. Oh yes, he has the best of everything, and I always feed him myself. Yet he's jumped the garden wall twice lately and run away. The police brought him back on both occasions. I don't know what to do . . .'

'He *seems* fond of you,' I said. Chum, who had a blunt, foolish face, was gazing up at him sentimentally.

'Yes, he is, you know,' said the gentleman, brightening a little. 'That's the funny part of it. He's as pleased as Punch to see me when I come home—sometimes he won't eat his dinner till I've left him, no matter how hungry he is; yet the next minute he buzzes off. I've made a run for him in the garage now; well, I can't trust him alone in the garden any more, and the wife's got enough to do already without having to keep an eye on him. She's not that keen on dogs, anyway. Fact is, I'm afraid he may be a bit lonely, for I can't spend as much time with him now as I did before I married, and I've been wondering whether he mightn't settle down better if I found *him* a wife, too.'

Was ever wish so miraculously granted! I at once described my own problem with Tulip, and Mr. Plum, as we will call him, for such he seemed to be, positively begged me to bring her along to his place on the following Saturday afternoon: his engagements unfortunately precluded him from inviting us earlier. Mr. Plum's place was off Putney Hill.

'Now do try to be serious!' I said to Tulip as, with a tin of vaseline in my pocket, I rang Mr. Plum's bell. He at once emerged and led us to the garage, which was built onto the side of the house. Here Chum was discovered at home, lying on a heap of clean straw, surrounded by quantities of dog biscuits, in a huge wire-netting cage which had been constructed in that part of the garage which did not contain Mr. Plum's car. Uttering no bark, he welcomed us all, and particularly Tulip, into his lair. But, although the signs were momentarily encouraging, I apprehended almost at once that we were probably in for much the same sort of afternoon that we had spent at the Blandishes'. Tulip was friendlier to Chum than she had been to Max. She played and flirted with him a little, while, he on his side, though half Max's age and quite without experience, put up an infinitely better show than his predecessor. The warmth of his feelings was, indeed, plainly and frequently visible. But though he tried constantly to take her, awares and unawares, she slid out of his grasp every time and repulsed him. As before, her attention was fixed upon myself.

Mr. Plum was wonderfully kind and patient. He gave her presents and did what he could to placate her and to understand the cause of her nervous excitement. Might it not be a good idea, he asked, to leave them together for a bit? Perhaps Tulip would concentrate better if my distracting presence were removed, and (he looked at his watch) Mrs. Plum had a cup of tea for us in the flat. I did not think it at all a good idea, but, except for the matter of vaseline, which I now mentioned and which he said we must certainly try out later, had none better to offer, and a nice cup of tea, after the chill of the garage, would be most welcome. We accordingly edged our way out of the cage and shut the wire door. Thwarted in her attempt to push out with me, poor Tulip rose up frantically against it, while Chum tried in vain to take her in the midst of her woe.

The striking thing about Mr. Plum's flat was its cleanliness. The kitchen, into which I was led, was almost dazzling; it was more like a model kitchen in an Ideal Home Exhibition than a room actually lived in and used. Everything was spotlessly clean and tidy, everything shone, the blue and white enamel paint on the walls, the polished linoleum, the white wood table and pale blue chairs, the gleaming pots and pans; everything looked brand new, everything was neatly arranged in its proper place, not a speck of dust was to be seen. Except, reprehensibly one felt, in the shaft of wintry sunlight that fell from a high window and illumined, like a spotlight, the erect figure of the mistress of the house. A pretty, neat, unsmiling young woman, Mrs. Plum stood in the midst of her immaculate kitchen, holding in her arms the most doll-like baby I ever saw. Two cups of tea were already poured out. They stood, precisely placed, with a sugar bowl, on the table, and Mrs. Plum, inclining her head a little as I bowed to her, invited me to accept one. I thanked her and took it up. It was not tepid, it was cold. It must have been poured out for a quarter of an hour at least. From this I inferred that one had to enter into Mrs. Plum's scheme of things, that punctuality played an important part therein, and that we were late. Presumably Mr. Plum's tea was as cold as my own but he did not flinch. I then congratulated Mrs. Plum on the beauty of her kitchen, and added that it was a marvel to keep a place so clean when it contained a dog.

'He's not allowed into the house,' said she, in a grave voice. 'Dogs make things dirty.'

Throughout this short interlude Tulip's faint but heartrending cries had been audible from the garage. Unable to bear them any longer, I suggested to Mr. Plum that we should return and see how the courtship was progressing—though I was under no illusion that her cries were due to physical pain. He agreed, and when I had thanked Mrs. Plum for her delightful hospitality we made good our escape.

Tulip was exactly where we had left her, by the wire door, though now sitting down, presumably for safety's sake, while Chum hovered wearily in the background. For the next half-hour we did our best to effect a conjunction between them. I smeared Tulip lavishly with vaseline and tried to hold her still while Mr. Plum strove to guide Chum, whom fatigue had made erratic, to a more accurate aim. But it was all of no use. Tulip either squirmed her posterior aside or sat down upon it, and at length began to appeal to me with such obvious distress, uttering quavering, beseeching cries and rising up to lick my face, that I realized that our efforts to please had turned into cruelty and said we must stop. Mr. Plum, sweet fellow, at once agreed. But we were both of us disappointed and perplexed. What was Tulip trying to tell us? Had I lost her ready time? Had I brought her to Max too early and to Chum too late? Was neither dog personally acceptable to her? Or did she simply not know what to do? Or was her devotion to myself all the love she needed? Or could it be, as Mr. Plum suggested, that the *mise-en-scène* was unpropitious and that she might relax more if the action were transferred to my own flat? This was a characteristically sensitive thought, and when he then offered to bring Chum to call upon Tulip next day I accepted with gratitude.

The most conspicuous result of Mr. Plum's visit was that my flat was rapidly transformed into a condition which, had it been her place, would have caused Mrs. Plum instantly to swoon away. A thaw had set in, and although I foresaw the consequences of this and did what I could to protect my carpets from the forthcoming invasion by laying sheets of newspapers over them, I need not have troubled myself. Tulip greeted Chum with infantile pleasure and at once instituted nursery games, romping with him on my large, now messy, terrace, and then chasing him, or being chased by him, in and out of the flat, scattering the newspapers like leaves in the wind. He still found her attractive, but of sexual interest on her side there was no sign.

Later on we took them out for a walk together on Putney Common. It was a fine day and an agreeable expedition, though more agreeable to me than to Mr. Plum, for the contrast in behavior of our two animals was now too plainly seen. Chum soon got bored with Tulip's scoldings and flew constantly off in pursuit of other dogs, paying no attention at all to Mr. Plum's commands, while Tulip kept a vigilant eye upon me and deferred to my opinion about everything she did. Poor Mr. Plum observed her with envy.

'I thought Chum was going to be like that,' said he, 'but—well, I don't like to blame him, I've a feeling I let him down. I'm fond of walking, and we've had some jolly good hikes together, but of course when you're married you've got other people to consider. This Sunday walk's his weekly treat now, not that I wouldn't take him out more often, especially of a summer's evening, but you can't always please yourself when you're married, and it's natural, after all, that the wife should want one's company too. Chummy! Chummy!' But Chummy had vanished. 'There you are, you see . . .'

When we had retrieved him, I said:

'It's a pity you can't have him with you in the flat. After all, dogs do like company and to busy themselves about their masters.'

Mr. Plum sighed:

'Yes, I'm afraid he mopes. And of course I'd love to have him in with me like I did in my bachelor days, but, well you know what women are, house-proud and so on, and I can quite see the place would get a bit mucky, not that I should mind that . . .'

But I had left off listening to Mr. Plum's sorrowful reflections. Cutting across our path was a curious figure who instantly caught my attention. This was a rough, thick-set man with the cauliflower ears and battered face of a pugilist. He was wearing a roll-necked sweater and a tiny cap. What riveted my interest upon him, however, was the fact that he was being hauled along by two powerful young Alsatian dogs on a chain. A boy walked at his side. To let such a man pass at such a moment would have been to fly in the face of providence, and I accosted him. He was readily conversable. Yes, he knew all about Alsatians, he bred them as a sideline to his work, and these two splendid young dogs who were trying to get at Tulip, had been reared by him. Craving his indulgence, I described my perplexities and requested his valuable advice. He studied Tulip with a beady eye.

'I wouldn't be surprised,' he then remarked darkly, 'if she's a barren bitch.'

'Barren!' I cried. 'How can you tell?'

'Ah, I'm not laying it down, but that'd be my guess.

Too nervous and 'ighly strung for my liking. But if you showed me 'er pedigree I could tell from that.'

'I haven't got it on me,' I said dejectedly.

'Well, you could fetch it along some other time. Any road, I reckon 'e wouldn't stand much chance with 'er,' he continued, casting at Chum a disparaging glance. 'Too young and flimsy, if you take my meaning. Now if it 'adn't been a Sunday and so many people about and me 'aving the young lad with me an' all, I wouldn't 'ave minded unleashing one of me own dogs on 'er, 'ere and now. They'd soon find out if she was a barren bitch or not!'

'But isn't it too late in her season? It must be her fourteenth or fifteenth day.'

'Seeing as 'ow she's carrying on with that there mongrel,' he replied, 'I'd say she could still be done. And if I was you, I'd watch out!'

'Tulip!' I said reproachfully.

We had been followed for some time by a small dog, one of those smooth, tight-skinned, busy and bouncing little creatures who, if dogs wore hats, would certainly have worn a bowler. He had attached himself to Tulip in very nearly the closest sense of the word, and was receiving from her all those marks of favor which she had declined to bestow upon Max or Chum. Indeed, she was clearly vastly amused by this artful little dodger, who was making repeated attempts to jump her, an ambition which I had already been pondering whether he was too small to achieve, and although she skipped her bottom from side to side when I admonished her, she was accepting from him, with an appearance of absent-mindedness, a shameful amount of familiarity. Our oracle observed all this with interest.

'Aye,' said he, 'I believe she'd stand for that little bloke where she wouldn't stand for Chum; and if she'd stand for *'im,* she would't get away from *my* dogs once they'd got a grip on 'er.'

All this was extremely tantalizing.

'There aren't really many people about,' I said. 'Can't we go over into those bushes? No one would see us there.'

'I'm right sorry to disoblige you. I'd 'ave been pleased to try; but I couldn't do that, not in front of the young lad.' Then, lowering his voice to a hoarse whisper, he asked: 'Did you give 'er a lead at all? You know, prompt 'er, like? There's ways of stimulating 'em up.'

'Vaseline?' I murmured.

'Ah, you knew about that,' said our bruiser disappointedly, and turned to Mr. Plum. 'You can stimulate Chum up, too. Did you know? In case you're thinking of putting them together again next time.' Chum had never seemed to me in need of stimulation, but Mr. Plum assumed a suitably vacant expression and shook his head. 'That's a pity. It's simple, but it's quite a tip. And I wouldn't 'ave minded demonstrating it on one of me own dogs, if it 'adn't been for the presence of the young lad.'

I had by now conceived so intense a dislike for this sickly-faced youth who, with his yellow complexion and puffy eyes, looked as though there was little he did not already know, at any rate about the art of self-stimulation, that I could hardly keep the venom out of my gaze, and asked irritably whether he could not be sent for a walk by himself. The desire to instruct is a powerful one, and our lecturer could not resist it. He accordingly sent the boy off with one of the dogs, and then, after a cautious look round, demonstrated upon the remaining animal what occurred when one took its member into the palm of one's hand and exerted a slight warming pressure. What occurred requires no further enlarging upon; and after this interesting lesson we took his address and our leave, and that was the end of my first attempt to marry Tulip.

Mr. Plum saw us home and I invited him up for a glass of sherry; but although he was clearly tempted, he thought, after studying his watch, that he had better not, it might make him late for his Sunday dinner, and, well, you know, when one was married that didn't do. I had already learnt that it didn't do to be late for tea, so I did not press him and he hurried off, this good, kind, once adventurous, now lost young man to his doom, while I ascended in the elevator with mine.

4 · Journey's End

*I*f there were lessons to be drawn from this failure to mate Tulip, I was far from certain what they were. With plenty of leisure now, a full six months, in which to prepare for the next event, I felt I should have been in a position to profit from experience and plan something better. But the only concrete fact that seemed to have emerged was that the vet who had said that mating dogs was not as easy as one might think had not exaggerated. Perhaps it would be safer, after all, to hand the business over to professionals, and I went so far as to answer the advertisement of one of them, the owner of a stud dog of great fame, not only for the antiquity of his lineage, but also for the number of decorations he had won for gallantry on the field of battle, and made a short journey with Tulip into Surrey to see this noble beast, whose name was Sultan and whose semen cost ten guineas.

In order to save us the additional trouble of a bus ride to his house, the owner had agreed to meet me at the station. Since it was a Sunday morning before opening time, our confabulation, such as it was, took place in the station yard. It was disappointing. He brought with him only a photograph of his distinguished animal; Sultan himself had had a busy Saturday, he said, and was feel-ing rather tired; and although it was of no great impor-tance that I should see him, I had that mild curiosity which most of us feel to view celebrities in the flesh—or the fur. Moreover, since pedigree Alsatians are always photographed in the same position and attitude, side-ways, with their tails down, their heads up, and one hind leg in advance of the other, they all look to my inexpert eye pretty much the same. However, I enjoyed chatting to my breeched and gaitered friend about dear Tulip's sexual problems, and took from him the impression I was growing accustomed to receive from professional people in the dog world, that he regarded me as imper-fectly right in the head. But I minded this less than the view he took of Tulip, whom he described as 'rather too long in the barrel.' Nevertheless, I was glad to have his assurances that I had only to phone him and he would bring Sultan to Putney any day, at any time, and at the shortest notice. I do not think I ever seriously intended to avail myself of Sultan's services, but it was nice to know that I might do so if I wished. I wanted as many rods in the next fire as I could muster; but at the same time there seemed to me—I had felt it all along—something unnatural about bringing two dogs, total strangers, together for an hour or so for the purpose of copulation, not to mention having to stimulate them into taking an interest in each other. I perceived that I might be influenced in this feeling by the fact that my royal bitch was, of course, so infinitely superior to anything else in her domesticated species that she seemed scarcely to belong to it at all. I perceived, too, or thought I perceived, the danger of translating human emotions into beastly breasts. But whether or not my recent fiasco with Tulip could be attributed to such personal causes, that neither of her two suitors had been attractive to her, there was no doubt that in normal times she displayed decided preferences in her canine relationships. There were two or three mongrels in my district for whom she had a special fancy; to one in particular she was so devoted that it was quite a romance. It was even quite a menace. Ordinarily far less interested in dogs than in many other things, and possessed of an exemplary road sense, she was nevertheless liable to cross the street, without permission or precaution, if she perceived this favorite of hers upon the other side. He was a very small and rather wooden terrier, with a mean little face streaked black-and-white like a badger, and I had only to pronounce his name, which was Watney, for her to prick up her ears and lead me excitedly to the public house in which he lived. Hastening across the Saloon Bar to the counter, she would stand up on her hind legs and peer over it to see if he was there. The publican, who was privy to the romance, would let the little dog out, and Tulip would greet him with all her prettiest demonstrations of pleasure, curtsying down to him on her elbows in her play attitude, with her rump and its waving tail up in the air. Every now and then, as he rotated around her, she would place a paw on his back as though to hold him still for contemplation.

What she saw, or smelt, in this dreary little dog I never could understand. Disillusioned women often upbraid their husbands with: 'You only like me for one thing!' and this might well have been the case between Tulip and Watney. During her heats he practically lived on our doorstep and, when she appeared, clung like a limpet to one of her hind legs—he could reach no higher—while she patiently stood and allowed him to do with her as he would and could. But when, in the long intervals between, she visited him in his pub in all her fond and radiant beauty, he never found for her more than a moment to spare. Having trotted round her once and ascertained, with a sniff, that there was nothing doing, he would retire stiffly on his apparently hingeless legs to his duties behind the bar (he guarded the till and rang the bell at closing time)—duties which he totally neglected when she was in season—leaving her sitting, frustrated and forlorn, in the Saloon.

'Never mind, Tulip dear,' I would say, as she turned her mournful gaze upon me. 'It's the way of the world, I fear.'

The nicest thing for her, therefore, it seemed to me—assuming she was not a barren bitch—would be to find her an Alsatian Watney. It was possible, of course, that Sultan himself might be that very person and that she would take instantly to him—love at first smell; but gratifying though this would be in one way, such a coincidence would also suggest that if I had only persevered in my search I might have found at last, by trial and error, some other instantly acceptable and less costly husband.

But when I shelved Sultan in my mind and took stock of my alternatives, the prospect was not rich. There was, in fact, only one hopeful line, and on a Sunday morning in the spring I set out with Tulip and her pedigree to call on my bruiser friend.

'Everyone knows me,' he had said. 'You just ask where Chick lives when you're down my way and anyone'll tell you.'

It was a working-class street and a small untidy house; Chick, who was engaged in his back garden, where kennels and vegetables sprouted together, received us there cordially. But alas, his circumstances had changed; he had sold both his dogs and had nothing left but the old bitch, their mother. Nor did his examination of Tulip's pedigree, which he studied attentively, tracing the strains in her blood with a thick dirty finger and every now and then wheezing out a foreboding 'Ah!', provide the decisive answer to the question of her barrenness which he had led me to expect. But the visit was not entirely negative, for he gave me some advice. A talkative man who liked to have an audience, his successful hobby of dog-breeding—some of his dogs had won prizes—had brought him into contact with notable people. There were frequent allusions to Major this and Colonel that, other luminaries in the breeding world of whom he was surprised and pained to find I had never heard:

'Well, they all know Chick. If you bump into them you just mention my name. You won't need no more introduction than that.'

The particular advice he gave me was never to send Tulip to kennels for mating. This, of course, was another possibility that had vaguely crossed my mind; it was what so many of my acquaintances seemed to do. But he spoke very strongly against it. All sorts of things went on in kennels that weren't right, he said, when he had sent the young lad back into the house to give Mum a hand with the Sunday dinner; breeding was a profitable business, so bitches had to be bred from whether they liked it or not; if they weren't willing they were helped, if they wouldn't be helped they were forced, and many a time he'd seen them muzzled and put into a sling to prevent them resisting. All this was very bad, said he, especially for nervous bitches like he reckoned Tulip to be . . . The advice pleased me, it chimed with my own ideas; yet as I walked her away I reflected that this beautiful animal had herself been born in a kennel and had therefore, perhaps, been conceived in this very way.*

It was during this time that Miss Canvey re-entered my life, and I carried my problem to her. She was immediately helpful. She had two or three Alsatian-owners

---

* Nevertheless she is degenerate. She cannot digest hard bone. Inbreeding has deprived her of the powerful gastric juices she should have. Bone remains in her stomach or reaches her gut almost unchanged, she screams when she tries to defecate and has to be quickly taken to a vet for an enema.

on her books whom she was willing to approach; but she added what seemed to me a far more satisfactory proposition: her own kennel-maid possessed an Alsatian, named Timothy, of whom I could have the use, a possible advantage of this choice being, said Miss Canvey, that she herself would supervise the operation. On the other hand, it had to be admitted, Timothy, though 'quite good,' was not a highly-bred dog, and perhaps I ought to see him before making up my mind. But my mind was already made up. What could be better than to hand the whole thing over to dear Miss Canvey? I inspected Timothy nevertheless. He was the smallest Alsatian I had ever seen, no larger in height and build than Tulip herself; but he was nicely shaped in his small-scale way and had an extremely intelligent face. He was reputed to be as devoted to his mistress as Tulip was to me, which may have explained why, when the two animals were given a preliminary opportunity to meet, they took of each other no notice whatever. But never mind, the matter was now in Miss Canvey's capable hands. She told me to phone her as soon as Tulip's heat began, and with everything so ideally arranged I gave up hunting for other dogs.

On August 22, spots of blood appeared again on Tulip's shins and I phoned the news to Miss Canvey. When should I bring her along? Miss Canvey at once supplied the clue I had missed in the autumn:

'Bring her as soon as she starts to hold her tail sideways when you stroke her.'

Wonderful Miss Canvey! No other vet, nor any dog book I had ever read, had thought fit to provide this inestimably important piece of information, a truth, like many another great truth, so obvious in its simplicity when it is pointed out that I wondered how I could have failed to notice it before and draw from it its manifest conclusions. Tulip herself supplies the answer to the question of her readiness. At the peak of her heat, from her ninth or tenth day, her long tail, as soon as she is touched anywhere near it, or even if a feint of touching her is made, coils away round one flank or the other, leaving the vaginal passage free and accessible. This pretty demonstration of her physical need goes on for several days; during all of these she is receptive.

I took her down to Miss Canvey on September 1. The arrangement was that I should leave her there on my way to work and call for her on my return. There was a stable-yard attached to Miss Canvey's old-fashioned establishment, and there the two animals were to spend the intermediate hours together, under observation from the surgery windows. Tulip evinced no particular pleasure at meeting Timothy again; her desolate cries followed me as I left. When I rejoined her in the evening I was told that he had penetrated her but had not tied.* This, I gathered, had not been achieved without help. Miss Canvey was displeased and asked me to fetch her back in a couple of days for another go. On this second occasion, again with help, the animals tied for ten minutes, and Miss Canvey declared herself satisfied. After a lapse of three weeks I was to produce Tulip for examination. I did so. She was not pregnant. She was not to be a mother after all.

This was the end of my second attempt to mate her, and since it had seemed successful, it was a greater dis-

---

* Or locked. The dog's penis only reaches full erectal size after entering the bitch. It cannot then be withdrawn until detumescence occurs. Foxes and wolves have the same coital pattern.

appointment than the first. Was it a confirmation of Chick's dark suspicion? Miss Canvey thought not: Tulip was a little narrow in the pelvis but seemed otherwise perfectly normal, she said. She was deeply apologetic and offered to try again in the autumn if I had no better prospects. But my mind was in as great a muddle as ever. I did not know, of course, what had gone on in the stable yard, for I had not been present; but it seemed to me on reflection that I had come pretty close to those stud practices which Chick had deprecated and I had intended to avoid. Miss Canvey was the kindest of women and a qualified vet; she must know far more about these things than I did; yet my questioning mind remained doubtful. Doubtful and now distressed. Call it 'helped,' call it what one would, my virgin bitch had been ravished, it seemed to me, without spontaneity, without desire, and I could not believe that that was right.

Then I came across a book, *The Right Way to Keep Dogs*, by Major R. C. G. Hancock, which formulated and confirmed all my suspicions. The importance of wooing in a bitch's sex life, he says, cannot be over-estimated. Though she will not consent to consummate the act of mating during the first week of her heat, 'she is strongly attractive during this wooing period to all the males of the pack, who follow her in a hopeful procession, fighting amongst themselves from time to time to settle the primacy of approach. The result is that by the second week, when the bitch allows mating to take place, she had gone through a process of strenuous wooing, so that the ovaries have been stimulated to shed a large number of eggs into the womb, there to await fertilization.' He then repeats much of what Chick had told me. 'Only those familiar with the breeding technique of the present-day pedigree breeder will know how far their methods negate this natural certainty. The bitch is kept shut up during the week when she should be the object of constant wooing and stimulus by the male. On the day she is adjudged ready for mating, she is taken and held, often muzzled, while the precious stud dog, lest he be injured, is carefully lifted into position. Under these circumstances, with no love-making precedent to the act, both sexes are indolent in performance, eggs are few in number, and the male seed poor in quality and quantity. In many cases the "tying" of the dog to the bitch is not effected because of this sexual indolence. No wonder the resulting litter is small or non-existent . . . If possible, let them have a run out together daily during the first week. When one or other parent has never mated before, this is particularly important to allow the subconscious instincts to organize themselves, and, by trial and error, the technique of mating becomes possible. I have seen many virgin males introduced to a bitch ready for mating, and the dog, though showing every sign of desire, just does not know what is expected of him.'

Since these passages described, with an accuracy so startling that I wondered for a moment whether their author had been shadowing me, everything that had happened to Tulip, I could hardly do other than accept them as truth. If she was not barren I had simply muddled two of her heats away. Yet it was all very well! Reconsidering Major Hancock's counsel of perfection, how was I to organize a large pack of pedigree Alsatians to pursue and fight for her during the first week of her heat? And where was this interesting scene to be staged? No doubt it was a splendid idea, but difficult to arrange. Failing that, the implication seemed to be that if she had seen a good deal more of Max, Chum and Timothy from the beginning they would have stood a better chance. Well, perhaps. . . . But was it true to say that she had gone to any of them unwooed and unstimulated? Admittedly they had not wooed her themselves, but she had had the prior attention of quantities of Putney mongrels on all these occasions, so that if followers and their wooings fertilized the womb, hers should have been positively floating with eggs before she met any of her prospective mates.

Indeed, during this second wasted season, both before and after Timothy's failure, I had a lot of trouble with the local dogs, far more than I had had in the winter. Theoretically, Tulip was perfectly welcome, so far as I was concerned, to canine company at these times, so long as it was the right company. The right company depended upon the period. At the onset and decline of her oestrus I did not mind what company she kept, for it seemed safe to assume that she was unconsenting, if not impenetrable, during the first six and last six days of her cycle at least. Even between these dates I was still willing to permit followers, so long as they were too small, or too old, or too young, to be able to give and obtain any satisfaction greater than flattery. I felt, indeed, extremely sympathetic towards Tulip's courtiers (I would have been after the pretty creature myself, I thought, if I had been a dog); she clearly enjoyed being pleasured by their little warm tongues, and I wished her to have as much fun as she could get. But theory and practice seldom accorded. The dogs were scarcely ever the requisite size and age; moreover, they constantly abused my hospitality by persecuting her and each other. And of them, it seemed to me now, the little dog, to whom hitherto I had felt especially well-disposed, was far more tiresome (at any rate when he was plural, which he usually was) than his larger brethren, more lecherous, more persistent, and more quarrelsome.

'They are like the little men,' indignantly remarked a rather *passée* lady of my acquaintance to whom I recounted my woes; '*always* the worst!'

They took no hint, as the bigger dogs sometimes did, from the symbolic use of the lead when I kept Tulip on it, but sexually assaulted her at my very heels if they thought they could do so with impunity; and since there are degrees of littleness, it was often a question where to draw the line.

'Don't bank on physical improbabilities,' someone had warned me. 'Before you can say knife the blade is inserted!'

The determined hoppings and skippings of these dubious and pertinacious little creatures in particular, therefore, alarmed me when she was receptive and inconvenienced me in any case. It became quite a puzzle to know where to exercise her. Why exercise her at all at such a time? it may be asked—but only by those people who have never had my problem to contend with, the problem of confining an active, eager and importunate young bitch to a small London flat for three weeks. Difficult though it was to take her out, it was more exhausting and demoralizing to keep her in. This took on the terrible aspect of punishment, and how could I punish a creature for something she could not help and, moreover, when she herself was so awfully good? For even in heat Tulip gave me no trouble of any kind. Other bitches of my acquaintance, in a similar condition, whose owners had the resolution and the facilities—sheds, gardens, cellars—to shut them away out of sight and sound, were always on the watch for chances to escape, and sometimes found them, returning home only when they were pregnant and famished. But if I had opened my flat door to Tulip she would not have gone out of it alone; if I had taken her down into the street and put her with her friends, she would have left them to follow me back upstairs. The only fault I could find with her was that she was apt to spread the news of her condition by sprinkling the doorstep on her way in and out (a dodge I noticed at this time too late to prevent it), which naturally brought all the neighboring dogs along in a trice to hang hopefully about the building for the rest of her season. This, if she had been a rational creature, she would have seen to be short-sighted, for her walks, which she valued even now above all else, became thereafter as harassed as are the attempts of film stars and other popular celebrities to leave the Savoy Hotel undetected by reporters.

In the kindness and weakness of my nature, therefore, I took her out once or twice every day, and, in consequence, I fear, punished and upset her more than if I had kept her in. Our objective was usually the towing-path, not more than five minutes' walk away, and if only we could reach it unsmelt and unseen, or with, at most, a single acceptable companion, it offered a reasonable chance of peace, for town dogs seldom roam far from human habitations by themselves and such as we might meet would probably be in the control of their owners. Stealth, therefore, was an essential preliminary to success. I would spy out the land from my terrace, and, if the doorstep and Embankment approach to the towing-path were temporarily clear of enemy patrols, sally forth with Tulip on the lead (to prevent her from urinating

again), exhorting her *sotto voce* to silence. For a single
bark would undo us now: the locals, alerted for news of
her, would come flying helter-skelter from all points of
the compass. Bursting with excitement though she was,
she was usually wonderfully intelligent over this, and
would trot along soundlessly beside me, gazing up into
my face for guidance. Now we were on the Embankment, and only five hundred apparently dogless yards
separated us from our goal. How close the prize! How
seldom attained! As though some magical news agency
were at work, like that which was said to spread information among savage tribes, dogs would materialize out
of the very air, it seemed, and come racing after or towards us. And what a miscellaneous crew they were!
Some, like Watney, were so small that by no exertion or
stroke of luck could they possibly achieve their high ambition; some were so old and arthritic that they could
hardly hobble along; yet all deserted hearth and home
and, as bemused as the rats of Hamelin, staggered, shuffled, hopped, bounced and skirmished after us so far that
I often wondered whether those who dropped out ever
managed to return home. And now what did one do, with
a swarm of randy creatures dodging along behind with
an eye to the main chance, of which they had the clearest
view, snarling and squabbling among themselves for
what Major Hancock calls the 'primacy of approach,'
and provoking Tulip to a continual retaliation which
either entangled my legs in the lead or wrenched my
arm out of its socket?

I usually ended by doing two things. I released her
from the lead, which, since she might be said to live
always on a spiritual one, was more an encumbrance
than an advantage. Then I lost my temper. For it was

at this moment that her intelligence failed her. I would turn upon our tormentors with threatening gestures and shouts of 'Scram!', but before the effect, if any, of this could be gauged, Tulip, always ready to please, would assist me as she thought by launching herself vehemently at her escort. This, of course, defeated my purpose. It was precisely what I did not want because it was precisely what they wanted. They did not take her onslaughts at all seriously and, one might say, could scarcely believe their good fortune at finding her in their midst. Yet, command and yell at her as I did, I could not make her see that all I required of her was that she should remain passively at my side. Poor Tulip! With her bright, anxious gaze fixed perpetually on my stern face striving to read my will, many a curse and cuff did she get for being so irrepressibly helpful! And how could she be expected to understand? Most of these dogs were her friends, with whom, a few days ago, she had been permitted, even encouraged, to hobnob; now apparently they were in disgrace, yet although I seemed angry with them and to desire their riddance, I was angry with her too for implementing my wishes.

The same thing happened, when, threats failing, I took to pelting the dauntless creatures with sticks and clods. Tulip, accustomed to having things thrown for her to retrieve, instantly flew off to retrieve them, and earned another slap when she playfully returned with the stick in her mouth and sundry dogs clinging to her bottom. Whatever she did, in short, was wrong, and soon she herself was in such a state of hysterical confusion that she no longer knew what she did, but, with all the intelligence gone out of her eyes and succeeded by a flat, insensitive, mad look, would jump up at me to seize the

missile before I threw it, and even when I had nothing
to throw, tearing my clothes or my flesh with her teeth.
It was in these circumstances that she inflicted upon me
the only bad bite she ever inflicted on anyone, as I have
related earlier.

Most of our walks, therefore, ended in ill-temper, and
I was thankful to get home where a self-operating elevator raised us safely out of reach of our oppressors whose
baffled gaze observed our ascension from the doorstep.
This elevator was a boon, for they had not the reasoning
power to associate its upward trend with the staircase
opposite; they were led entirely by the nose, and since
there was no smell of Tulip on the stairs, which I was
careful never to use while she was in this condition, they
never used them either and, being unable to work the
elevator or to rise above themselves in any other way,
remained where they were. Ill-temper was then succeeded by remorse and anxiety. Apart from the injustice
of the punishments I had awarded poor Tulip, might not
these displays of rage and violence harm her in other
ways, make her, for instance, aggressive where she had
been friendly, so that she would continue to go for her
own kind under the impression that this was what I
wished her to do? In fact this did not happen, but I believe, from what I see of the effect of human folly on
other dogs, that it might have done so if a solution to my
difficulties had not at last been found.

In the months that followed this second failure to mate
Tulip my mind was ceaselessly engaged in planning for
the future, and soon I had three more suitors lined up
for her, all belonging to people with leisure to afford

them a proper courtship. I had not worked out the mechanics, but my intention was to let her make her own choice among these three. An unforeseen fate ruled otherwise.

The human emotions that brought about her change of residence from London to Sussex do not belong to this history, which concerns itself with the canine heart; but a few words of explanation are necessary. A cousin of mine, who had no fixed abode, had rented a bungalow in Ferring for the winter months. Aware that I had been looking in vain for holiday accommodation that would accept an Alsatian dog, she invited us down to stay. We went. Newly painted white with a broad blue band round it, like a ribbon round a chocolate box, 'Mon Repos' was a trim little place. It had a garden fore and aft which my cousin, whose knowledge of gardening was slender to the point of invisibility, had undertaken to 'keep up.' The front one contained a rockery with flowering shrubs, among which were tastefully disposed figurines of the Seven Dwarfs. It was quite the prettiest bungalow in Witchball Lane. That we had not, however, been invited entirely disinterestedly soon appeared: my cousin confessed to being nervous of staying in 'Mon Repos' alone. Arguments were therefore advanced, when the end of my holiday approached, for prolonging a situation that suited her: Tulip was enjoying herself, it was nice for her to have a garden to play in, and the walks round about were superior to anything that Putney had to offer; she was looking better already for the change; why not leave her there to profit from the wonderful sea air and come down myself at weekends to join her? The value of sea air to canine health was an idea that had not occurred to me, but I saw that there was some small sub-

stance in the rest of the argument. On the other hand I
did not want to be separated from Tulip throughout the
week and believed that all her present amusements com-
bined were as nothing to her anxiety not to be separated
from me; nor had I the slightest inclination to make a
railway journey to 'Mon Repos' every weekend. But
when women have set their hearts on something, the
wishes and convenience of others are apt to wear a
flimsy look; my own point of view, when I ventured it,
was quickly dismissed as selfishness. I was sorry for my
cousin and consented. I only stipulated that Tulip must
be removed to London before her next heat, which was
due in March. This was agreed to.

To recall the weeks that followed is no pleasure, but
since this is the story of Tulip's love life they should
not be passed over in silence. An alarm clock woke me
at 6:45 every Monday morning; I then had half an
hour in which to get up and catch the bus at the top of
Witchball Lane for the station a couple of miles away.
Tulip, who slept always in my room, would get up too
and follow me about as I tip-toed between bedroom,
bathroom and kitchen. I knew, without looking at her,
that her gaze was fixed unswervingly upon me, that her
tall ears were sharp with expectation. I knew that, the
moment she caught my attention, they would fall back
as though I had caressed her, then spring up again while
she continued to search my face with that unmeetably
poignant inquiry in which faith and doubt so tragically
mingled: 'Of course I'm coming with you—aren't I?'
Avoiding her eyes for as long as I could, I would go
about my preparations; but the disappointing had to be
done at last. As I picked up my bag in the bedroom, she
would make her little quick participating movement

with me through the door, and I would say casually, as though I were leaving her for only a moment, 'No, old girl, not this time.' No more was needed. She would not advance another step but, as if the words had turned her to stone, halt where she was outside the bedroom door. Now to go without saying goodbye to her I could not, though I knew what I should see, that stricken look, compounded of such grief, such humility, such despair, that it haunted me all the journey up. 'Goodbye, sweet Tulip,' I would say and, returning to her, raise the pretty disconsolate head that drooped so heavily in my hands, and kiss her on the forehead. Then I would slip out into the darkness of Witchball Lane. But the moment the door had closed behind me she would glide back into our bedroom, which was on the front of the bungalow, and rearing up on her hind legs at the window, push aside the curtains with her nose and watch me pass. This was the last I would see of her for five days, her gray face, like a ghost's face, at the window, watching me pass.

The year turned, the date of our departure drew near, and my cousin's mind got busy, as I guessed it would, with the problem of obstructing it. She really could not see the necessity for taking Tulip away. Why should she not have her heat in Ferring?

'Because I've fixed up her love affairs in Putney.'

'None of your dogs could possibly be as good as Mountjoy, and Mrs. Tudor-Smith is frightfully keen on the marriage.'

This was a high card. Mountjoy belonged to some people a little further down Witchball Lane. He was an Alsatian of such ancient and aristocratic ancestry that Mrs. Tudor-Smith had been heard to declare that his genealogy went back even further than her own. She had paid as much as a hundred guineas for the privilege of possessing him. He gave, indeed, in his appearance and manners, so instant a conviction of the bluest of blood that it would have been both superfluous and impertinent to ask to see his pedigree. More like a lion than a dog, with his magnificent tawny coat and heavy ruff, he was often to be viewed in the grounds of the bungalow in which he resided, or just outside its gates, standing always in the classic attitude as though he had invented it. Perpetually posing, it seemed, for cameras that were his customary due and were doubtless somewhere about, he gave the impression not so much of looking up or down Witchball Lane as of gazing out over distant horizons. He had neither any objection nor any wish to be stroked; he accepted caresses from strangers in the aloof manner in which a king might receive tribute from his subjects; when he felt he had done his duty by the human race, he would stalk majestically back into the house; and if he had ever emitted any sound louder than a yawn I had not heard it, certainly nothing so coarse as a bark. But it was not on account of his nobility that he was more advantageous than my Putney dogs; I was not greatly interested in the canine *Debrett;* it was simply that his situation with regard to Tulip made everything far easier. To get one animal to the other was a matter of only a minute's walk; they were already on friendly terms and often in each other's company.

I hesitated. Cashing in on this, my cousin added:

'If you want a second string, Colonel Finch says you can have Gunner whenever you like.'

During my weekends in Ferring I had met many of its dogs and their owners, and although Gunner was a far less impressive card than Mountjoy, he too was an

Alsatian and therefore eligible for Tulip's hand. Gunner
was an unlovable dog, as ill-favored as the hyena he
somewhat resembled and of bad local character. His
master, who doted on him, always averred that he was a
positive lamb and would not hurt a fly, but his habit was
to lie all day in the Colonel's porch on Ferring front and
charge out like the Light Brigade at every dog that
passed. Constant was the hot water into which Gunner
got his master. It was the commonest thing, as one walked
down the path by their bungalow, to hear the Colonel's
dominating voice on the further side of the hedge assur-
ing some other dog-lover, whose animal had just been
stampeded into the sea, that it was only Gunner's little
bit of fun. And, indeed, there may well have been some
truth in this, for the Colonel's own sense of humor was
of a similar cast, and since we are said to get like our
pets, perhaps *vice versa*, master and dog may have
grown to understand one another in an imitative kind of
way. The very first time I met Colonel Finch, he gave
Tulip an appraising look and rapped out at me:

'Hm! Pampered bitch, I can see! I bet she sleeps on
your bed!'

Much taken aback by this unprovoked attack, I confessed apologetically:

'I'm afraid she does. It's wrong, I suppose. Where
does Gunner sleep?'

'On the bed, of course!' roared the Colonel, delighted
to have teased me so successfully. 'The best bed in the
house!'

But Tulip failed to take of Gunner's 'little bit of fun'
the tolerant view I took of his master's. Having received
from him, as *their* first introduction, one of his famous
broadsides before he perceived her sex and attempted to

recover his mistake by a belated display of awkward gallantry, she never accorded him the condescension she showed to Mountjoy, and I did not therefore pin much hope on Colonel Finch's lamb. Nevertheless, with my resolutions now weakened—they needed little to under-mine them, for, in truth, I was not looking forward to Tulip's next heat—I said:

'In any case, you've no idea of the difficulties. You couldn't cope.'

'You're exaggerating,' said my cousin. 'If you can cope, so can I.'

Tulip entered her heat on the first of March, and even I never envisaged the consequences that rapidly de-veloped. Within a few days 'Mon Repos' was in a state of siege. My cousin began by thinking this rather amus-ing, and sent me cheerful accounts of the 'sweet' little Scotties and Sealyhams who had come to call. She found it less amusing when they accumulated and would not go away; when the larger dogs took to scrambling over the white-washed wall in front, which, by repeated leapings against the winter jasmine that had been carefully trained to ornament it, they could just manage to do; when their smaller associates, not to be outdone and left behind, contrived to smash the flimsy latch of the gate by constant rattling at it, and all camped out all night, quarrelling and whining, among the Seven Dwarfs. Nor did she find it amusing when the other ladies of Ferring, deprived of and anxious about their pets who returned not home even for their dinners, called round to retrieve them, not once but every day and a number of times a day, in a progressively nastier frame of mind. The soft answer that turneth away wrath is no part of the diplomatic equipment women claim to possess; my cousin was not one to be spoken to sharply without giving as good as she got. Very soon to the sound of Tulip's excited voice within and the replies of her devotees without was added a recurrent chorus of equally incontinent human voices raised in revilement and recrimination. And my cousin found it less amusing still when she tried to take Tulip for walks and fell into the error I had made of attempting to beat off her escort, which resulted not only in a more formidable incursion of enraged owners complaining that she had been seen ill-treating their pets, but, more affectingly, in her clothes and flesh getting torn. Before the first week was over, Tulip was not taken out at all; but now there was no lovely elevator to waft her out of sight, sound and scent of her admirers; good though she always was, no desirable and desiring bitch could be expected to behave with restraint in a small bungalow all the windows of which presented her with the spectacle of a dozen or so of her male friends awaiting her outside; she barked at them incessantly, hastening from window to window; they barked back; then, like the siren, she would break into song; the expensive net curtains were soon all in tatters, and these, in the end, I had to replace.

I could not replace 'Mon Repos' itself. By the close of the affair it is no exaggeration to say that it was practically wrecked. The walls still stood, of course; but what walls! A tepid rain had been falling for some time to add to the general melancholy of the scene, and their fresh white paint was liberally stippled with filthy paw marks where the excited creatures had tried to clamber in at the windows; the pale blue paint of the doors, at which they had constantly knocked, was scratched and scored; the Seven Dwarfs were prostrate in a morass that had once been a neat grassy border. Siege became invasion. The back of the bungalow held out a little longer than the front; its garden was protected by a fence; but as Tulip's ready time approached and the frustrated besiegers realized that this was where she now took the sea air, they set about discovering its weak spots. This did not take long. By the time I was able to come down for my second visit during this period, to stay now and supervise the marriage, they had already forced their way in at several points, and my cousin was hysterically engaged in ejecting dogs of all shapes and sizes from dining room, sun parlor and even in the night from her bedroom.

Into the midst of this scene of chaos Mountjoy, at the appropriate moment, was introduced. Tulip had not seen much of him during her wooing week; the Tudor-Smiths had thought it undesirable that he should mix in such low company; she was pleased to see him now. As soon as he made his wishes clear she allowed him to mount her and stood quietly with her legs apart and her tail coiled away while he clasped her round the waist. But, for some reason, he failed to achieve his purpose. His stabs, it looked to me standing beside them, did not quite reach her. After a little she disengaged herself, and assuming her play attitude, began to flirt in front of him. But he had graver ends in view. Again she stood, with lowered head and flattened ears, her gaze slanted back, apprehensively, I thought, to what he was doing behind. This time he appeared to have moved further forward, and now it did look as though he would succeed; but suddenly she gave a nervous cry and escaped from him once more. They tried again and again, the same thing always happened, whenever he seemed about to enter her she protested, as though she were still a virgin, and pulled herself free. And now it was quite upsetting to watch, his continual failure to consummate his desire and the consequent frustration of these two beautiful animals who wished to copulate and could not manage to do so. Nor could I see any way to help them, except to lubricate Tulip, which I did, for they seemed to be doing themselves all that could be done, except unite. It was, indeed, very moving, it was sorrow, to watch them trying to know each other and always failing, and it was touching to see Tulip give him chance after chance. But of course she was getting tired, she was panting; compared with him she was a small, slender creature, and it could not have been anything but burdensome for her to have the weight of his massive body upon her back and the clutch of his leonine arms about her waist. Yet, at the same time, he was as gentle with her as he could be; he took hold of her in a careful kind of way, or so it looked, manoeuvring his arms tentatively upon her as though to get a purchase that did not grip her too hard; and sometimes, when she made a nervous movement or uttered an anxious cry, he would dismount and, going round to her head, put his nose to hers as if to say: 'Are you all right?' But at last, in his own weariness, his jabs got wilder and wilder, quite wide of the mark; finally she would have no more to do with him and, whenever he approached her, drove him away.

Now what to do I did not know. Who would have supposed that mating a bitch could be so baffling a problem? Perhaps, in spite of her coiling tail, she was not ready. I set them together the following day, and the day after,

only to watch them go through the same agonizing performance. And now it was her twelfth day. Was there
truly something wrong with her, or was I muddling away
her third heat like the others? I sent for the local vet.
Next morning he came and stood with me while the animals repeated their futile and exhausting antics.

'It's the dog's fault,' he said. 'He can't draw.'

This term had to be explained to me. It meant that his
foreskin was too tight to enable him to unsheathe, a dis-
ability that could have been corrected when he was a
puppy. Besides this, the vet announced after examining
him, which Mountjoy permitted with extraordinary dignity, he was a 'rig' dog, that is to say he had an unde-
scended testicle, a not uncommon thing, said the vet, and
a serious disqualification in mating, since it was herita-
ble. It is scarcely necessary to add that neither of these
terms, nor any of this information, is mentioned in the
dog books, at least in none that I have ever come across.
Mountjoy's owners themselves, who had never offered
him a wife before, were totally ignorant of these facts,
if facts they were, and therefore of the corollary that
their noble and expensive beast was relatively worthless.

There was nothing now to be done but to phone Colonel Finch. In the late afternoon Tulip was hustled into a
taxi and conveyed to Gunner. Of the outcome of this I
never was in doubt and was not therefore disappointed.
She would have nothing to do with him at all. He was
willing, she was not; it was the bully's turn to be bullied,
and when the Colonel decided that his positive lamb had
had enough, Tulip reentered her taxi and was driven
back to 'Mon Repos.'

Dusk was now falling. I restored her to the ravaged garden, and it was while I stood with her there, gazing in

despair at this exquisite creature in the midst of her desire, that the dog-next-door emerged through what remained of the fence. He had often intruded before, as often been ejected. Now he hung there in the failing light, half in, half out of the garden, his attention fixed warily upon me, a disreputable, dirty mongrel, Dusty by name, in whom Scottish sheep-dog predominated. I returned the stare of the disconcertingly dissimilar eyes, one brown, one pale blue, of this ragamuffin with whom it had always amused Tulip to play, and knew that my intervention was at an end. I smiled at him.

'Well, there you are, old girl,' I said. 'Take it or leave it. It's up to you.'

She at once went to greet him. Dusty was emboldened to come right in. There was a coquettish scamper. She stood for him. He was too small to manage. She obligingly squatted, and suddenly, without a sound, they collapsed on the grass in a heap. It was charming. They lay there together, their paws all mixed up, resting upon each other's bodies. They were panting. But they looked wonderfully pretty and comfortable—until Tulip thought she would like to get up, and found she could not. She tried to rise. The weight of Dusty's body, united with her own, dragged her back. She looked round in consternation. Then she began to struggle. I called to her soothingly to lie still, but she wanted to come over to me and could not, and her dismay turned to panic. With a convulsive movement she regained her feet and began to pull Dusty, who was upside down, along the lawn, trying from time to time to rid herself of her incubus by giving it a nip. The unfortunate Dusty, now on his back, now on his side, his little legs scrabbling wildly about in their efforts to find a foothold, at length managed, by a kind of somersault, to obtain it. This advantage, however, was not won without loss, for his exertion turned him completely round, so that, still attached to Tulip, he was now bottom to bottom with her and was hauled along in this even more uncomfortable and abject posture, his hindquarters off the ground, his head down and his tongue hanging out. Tulip gazed at me in horror and appeal. Heavens! I thought, this is love! These are the pleasures of sex! As distressed as they, I hastened over to them, persuaded Tulip to lie down again for poor Dusty's sake, and sat beside them to caress and calm them. It was a full half-hour before detumescence occurred* and Nature released Dusty, who instantly fled home through the gap in the fence and was seen no more. As for Tulip, her relief, her joy, her gratitude (she seemed to think it was I who had saved her), were spectacular. It was more as though she had been freed from some dire situation of peril than from the embraces of love.

The following day I removed her to London and the haven of my flat. The house agent of 'Mon Repos' had been apprised of our activities and was belatedly on the warpath. Even my cousin had had enough. A car was summoned to take us to the station. When all was ready for immediate departure—the engine running, the car door open—I emerged from the ruined bungalow with Tulip on the lead and ran the gauntlet of dogs down the garden path. We rushed into the car, slammed the door, and were off. But the frenzied animals were not so easily

---

* It could have been longer.

balked. They pursued us in a pack so far down the country lanes that, though their number gradually dimin-
ished, I was suddenly terrified that the more pertinacious
would gain the station and invade the train. If there had
been any comedy in the situation ever, it was no longer
present; the scene had the quality of nightmare. But the
car outstripped them all at last and we got safely away.

5 · Fruits of Labor

*T*ulip was not a barren bitch. Three weeks after the events described I walked her over to Miss Canvey, who pronounced her pregnant. The tiny buds of her babes could already be felt in her womb. They were not Dusty's only gift to her. A persistent vaginal discharge, slight but noticeable, of a whitish color, also developed. Another visit to Miss Canvey was made. The discharge was politely termed a 'catarrh' due to an infection (recalling Dusty's raffish appearance I was not greatly surprised); though not considered dangerous to health, it had to be cleared up in case it miscarried the litter. Pills were provided and treacherously conveyed into Tulip's interior in pieces of meat. They did not work and were changed to bougies—hard, thin and pointed suppositories, two inches long, like half a short pencil—which I was told to insert into the vagina as far as my finger would go, so that they should not pop out again. Many a sorry struggle between Tulip and myself took place over these objects. Whenever she saw a bougie approaching she tucked her tail firmly between her legs and sought refuge on the bed, her back to the wall. From her piercing cries a few seconds later, anyone would have thought that I was doing her a mortal injury—and I began to wonder if I was. A third visit to Miss Canvey seemed advisable.

'Miss Canvey, I'm awfully sorry to bother you again, but where exactly is the vagina?'

'Forward and upwards,' said Miss Canvey briefly. 'Downwards leads to the bladder.' A furrow appeared on her brow. 'But I don't *think* you can be reaching *that*,' she added.

The struggles were resumed, with a little more confidence on my side, though none on Tulip's, but no bougies that I ever managed to insert stayed in for long. Flexible now but intact, they were discovered a minute or two later on carpet or bed, and attempts to reinsert them in their wobbly and slippery condition never succeeded though often made. Eventually my nerve failed me and

I begged Miss Canvey to put them in for me, which she did with enviable dexterity.

Apart from this unforeseen complication, little change was required to be made in Tulip's daily life. She was to be prevented from executing continuous rolls on the grass (which was not, in fact, a trick of hers), for the reason that a bitch's womb hangs in two lobes, like a medieval purse, and half the litter forms in each. The act of rolling, therefore, might cause the two lobes to intertwine and throttle each other.* Later on, when she got heavier, she was not to be asked to climb high steps, such as the steps of buses. Sixty-three days was the normal period of gestation, and bitches were said to be clocklike in their punctuality. She was therefore due to whelp on May 16.

As soon as the fact of her pregnancy was established my course of action became clear. Hitherto, the difficulties of allowing her to whelp in my flat had seemed insuperable; I had, indeed, been looking for a country kennel to which I could send her for her confinement. But from the beginning of my relationship with this enchanting beast I had more than once perceived that impossibilities tended to vanish as they were approached, and I knew now that I could not abandon her to strangers at this crisis of her life. Also I was immensely curious to see what happened.

I therefore set about designing a box for her. Not more care and thought were expended upon the building of the Ark than I gave to the construction of this box. I foresaw her needs as though they were my own: that it should have sufficient floor space to allow her to stretch

* A theory regarded by later veterinary opinion as fanciful.

out at full length comfortably on her side; that it should be high enough for her to stand up under its roof, and that it should be provided with a skirting board in front over which she, but not the puppies, could step, removable to facilitate cleaning. When the local carpenter, who had undertaken to make it out of odds and ends for a small sum, had finished it, I was aghast at its size, but it was somehow hauled up the four flights of stairs to my flat and installed, on layers of newspaper, in the darkest corner of my bedroom. At the bottom of it I laid an ancient raincoat, on this a wad of straw, on this again one of Tulip's blankets, for I had somewhere heard, and approved as sense, that bitches should not whelp in straw, which is liable to hamper them by getting mixed up with the umbilical cords of the litter.

The next thing was to habituate Tulip to the use of her box, so that she would go into it when the moment came. This prudent advice came from Miss Canvey. Since Tulip was accustomed to sleep on my bed, she said, she would probably whelp there unless I took precautions. Easier said than done. Tulip evinced a mild curiosity in the box when it arrived, and actually lay down in it for a few minutes in the evening, regarding me with an inscrutable expression over the skirting board. After that she took no further notice of it and, in spite of suggestions to the contrary, slept on my bed as usual. But in truth, I no longer cared what she did; I felt so tender towards the pretty pregnant creature that if she had chosen to whelp on my best suit of clothes I would not have chided her. However, I did not lay it out, and protected my bed to the extent of draping it with another old blanket.

For what seemed an incredible length of time she

showed no sign at all of the coming event. Then, quite suddenly, I observed the swell and sag of her belly and, in the first days of May, she began to flag and to take rests during our walks. This touched me. Hitherto, it had always been I who had sometimes felt fatigued, while she with her impatient high spirits had forced and teased me on; now it was she who could not stay the course. Soon Putney Common was as far as she could go, and even on these short strolls she would quietly halt and sink down upon the cool grass. Stretching myself beside her, I would smoke and read until she felt able to continue. A fortnight or so before she was due I asked Miss Canvey to be on hand in case we needed her, for bitches occasionally get into difficulties at their lying-in and require veterinary assistance.

But Tulip took us unawares. She whelped five days before her scheduled time and was alone in my flat when her labor began. The great unstaling pleasure of returning home was the welcome that she never failed to give me; there was no welcome that afternoon when I turned my key in the lock. The place was deathly, like a tomb. I hurried along to my bedroom. For some days I had been keeping the curtains there drawn; she would prefer, I knew, a dark, cool seclusion when her pains started. Standing now in the open doorway, I looked into the penumbrous room.

Tulip was in her box. She had understood its purpose after all. She was lying there in the shadows facing me, the front of her body upright, the rest reclined upon its side. Her ears crumpled back with pleasure at the sight of me; her amber eyes glowed with a gentle, loving look. She was panting. A tiny sound, like the distant mewing of gulls, came from the box, and I could just discern, lying against her stomach, three small rat-like shapes. I think it is Major Hancock who says that a bitch is liable to hold up her labor if she is distracted or watched, and may even devour her children to protect them. I accepted this in a general way; I knew, at the same time, that Tulip was glad that I was there. Nevertheless, I did not approach her box. Moving to a chair at some distance from her, I hid my face in my hands and observed her without seeming to do so. Suddenly she stopped panting, her face took on a look of strain, she uttered a muted, shuddering sound like a sigh, a movement passed over her recumbent body, and she raised her great tail so that it stood out straight and rigid from her rump. Immediately a dark package was extruded beneath it, and to this, with a minimum of general effort, she brought her long nose round. Now I could not clearly see what she was doing, for her head interposed and obscured the operation; but I knew what was happening and I heard her tongue and teeth at work with liquid guzzling noises. She was licking and nosing this package out of herself, severing the umbilical cord, releasing the tiny creature from its tissues and eating up the after-birth. In a few seconds she had accomplished all these tasks and was guiding her fourth child to her teats, cleansing it on the way.

It was a marvellous sight, to me very affecting; but I think that to anyone who did not know and love her as I did, it must have been a solemn and moving thing to see this beautiful animal, in the midst of the first labor of her life, performing upon herself, with no help but unerringly, as though directed by some divine wisdom, the delicate and complicated business of creation. I guessed now that she was thirsty. Quietly leaving the room, I warmed some milk for her. When I returned with the bowl she stretched her head eagerly forward. Kneeling in front of her, I held it to her while she lapped. She licked my hand and laid her head heavily back on the blanket.

Half an hour elapsed before her next delivery; then another sigh, another spasm, and her tail lifted to eject the fifth. She produced eight puppies at half-hourly intervals and was not done until evening fell. I sat with her in the darkened room throughout. It was a beautiful thing to have seen. When it was plain that she had finished I went and kissed her. She was quite wet. She allowed me to touch her babies. They were still blind. I took one up; she was frightened and gently nuzzled my hand as though to say 'Take care!' But she had too much confidence in me to suppose that I would hurt them.

It was misplaced. In the bathroom, as soon as my common senses returned and I envisaged a future that contained eight extra dogs, I prepared a bucket of water and a flour sack weighted with such heavy objects as I could lay my hands on. Following the trends of Hindoo social philosophy and the information I had gleaned that bitches were more difficult to get rid of than dogs, I quickly decided that the female part of Tulip's progeny, if only I could identify it from its sketchy hieroglyphics and—a graver problem still—abstract it without her knowledge, had better be instantly liquidated. I had read somewhere that animals cannot count, and that a cat with four kittens in a burning house, having removed all four to safety, will always return to reassure herself that there is not one left. How could I distract proud Tulip's attention while I carried out my dark deed? Soon, no doubt, she would wish to relieve nature and my chance would come. Soon she did. But the great confidence I have said she reposed in me was not now evident. Suddenly vacating her box, she hurried out into the passageway as though making for my terrace, which was her customary latrine. This was only a few yards further on, but to reach it involved a right-angle turn and letting her box out of her sight. Was it for this reason that she made no attempt to reach it? Had she read, as my guilty conscience supposed, the fell purpose in my eyes? Or was it simply that after all the strain she had endured and the unusual diet of quantities of warm milk and eight placentae, she was incontinently taken short? At any rate, she went no further than the passage. Swivelling herself round there in the open doorway so that her box was under her observation throughout, she squatted down on my Chinese carpet and let fly from both orifices simultaneously. Having rapidly squirted out large pools of No. 1 and No. 2, she flew back into her box, rearranged her children at her breast and directed at me a look of sympatthy over the skirting board. For the first time in her life she had deliberately fouled my flat. But I was not thinking of that as I mopped it all up. I was thinking how sadly bedraggled and thin she had appeared in the brief glimpse I had had of her.

The bucket and flour sack were fated not to be used, though looking back now over the years, it might have been better if they had been. Dear Miss Canvey, visiting soon afterwards with her scissors in search of dew-claws, said reprovingly:

'Why destroy any? They are nice puppies and she can easily manage the lot.'

What *she* could manage was not actually the question

that had been troubling me; but we are always glad to receive even irrelevant advice against doing the reasonable things we do not want to do, just as we are apt to brush aside as insubstantial the most cogent arguments when we are already determined upon some wrong-headed course of action. The female and, as it turned out, most refractory part of Tulip's litter was therefore reprieved.

For a month she was the perfect mother. Enchanting to watch in her concern for and pride in her offspring, she tirelessly cleaned up after them, swabbing their little posteriors when they defecated or piddled—in itself a non-stop task—and eating up all their excreta. It was wonderfully pretty to see her reclining there, while her children scrambled and pushed for her teats, looking down maternally at them with her great ears cocked forward, nosing among them the moment she smelt the odor of ordure, sorting out the guilty one, rolling it over onto its back with her sharp black nose and, disregarding its protesting squeals, vigorously licking its parts until they were clean. In spite of her vigilance, however, the blanket on which they lay soon got drenched, and I would change it for her daily, removing the puppies in a basin to some temporary abode, an event that always put her in a great taking. Twice a day too, on Miss Canvey's instructions, I took her for a short walk to afford her a brief respite from nursing. She came when I called her, though reluctantly, barking her anxiety all the way down in the elevator: two or three hundred yards along the Embankment were as far as she would ever go. Halting then in a resolute manner, she would challenge me to take another step; I would turn, and home she would hasten as fast as she could without actually deserting me, looking back at me all the time as though to say 'How you lag!', fly up the stairs (she could wait for no elevator), scratch impatiently at the door (I could not be quick enough with my keys), and race down the passage to rejoin her infants.

Then she began to get bored. Their rapidly increasing size and insatiable appetites put a strain on her of course; when they added to all this the growth of little pricking teeth she started to abdicate. Suddenly, while the now quite hefty children fought and elbowed each other aside to get at her most rewarding teats, she would rise to her feet and, with three of four of them who had got a better grip than the rest suspended like straphangers beneath her, emit one of those noisy, cavernous yawns that Alsatians are so good at, disembarrass herself of her encumbrances with a stretch and a shake, vault lightly out of the box and retire to the divan in my sitting-room for a peaceful doze, leaving a chorus of shrill dismay behind her. With the onset of her boredom came the onset of my own, for the less she fed them the more I had to. Also they began to wish to see the world and the skirting board no longer contained them. Clambering upon each other's backs in the middle of the night, they would fall headlong over the edge and set up a plaintive, incessant wailing until I woke and returned them to the fold. Soon afterwards they would do it again. All creatures have different characters and it is reasonable to suppose that some will be smarter than others; two of the four little bitches in Tulip's family were the first to climb out of the box and the most persistent in doing so. With lack of sleep my temper began to fray.

Converting my small dining room into a pen by removing the carpet and tacking chicken wire to the legs of
the furniture, I transferred my guests to that. It was no
time before, still led by the two little bitches, they were
dragging down or burrowing under these barriers too.
Their third and last arena was my open-air terrace,
where my double concern was to rig up contraptions
which would prevent them from reentering the flat or
crawling between the balusters of the balustrade to fall
sixty feet into the road below. These contraptions, too,
they seemed endlessly bent on demolishing. They were
charming, whimsical little creatures; they were also positively maddening, and exasperated me to such an extent
that I sometimes gave them a cuff for disobedience and
made them squeak, which was both an unkind and a useless thing to do, for they could not know what obedience
was. Tulip, on these occasions, would hurry out from her
dolce far niente to see what was afoot; she had practically abandoned them, but still took a proprietary interest in their welfare.

Also in their food. On Miss Canvey's instructions I
was now wearing myself out supplying the hungry stomachs with four meals a day, mixing milk dishes, where
there was no milk,* out of babies' milk powder (pro-
cured on false pretences from various chemists) and
Robinson's Patent Oats or Barley. Tulip, who had her
daily pound of horse-flesh, would come yawning and
stretching from her repose and gently insert her own
head among those of her children. Naturally a few laps
of her large tongue sufficed to scoop up most of the warm
liquid before her jostling brood (who got actually into

---

* The year was 1948.

the dish in their anxiety and paddled about) had managed to suck more than a drop from the rapidly sinking surface. Soon a soldier diet was prescribed, trenchers of carefully boned fish or minced raw horse-meat, mixed with wheat flakes and broken rusk. . . .

As they ate they grew; as they grew they waxed more eloquent. They began to growl and to utter little barks as they lurched about the terrace on their unsteady legs in that apparently purposeful but ultimately disastrous way drunks move, squabbling, playing tug-of-war and pulling one another's tails. Tulip herself would have a game with them when she felt disposed, plant her large paws on them like a cat with a mouse, or race up and down the terrace in front of them, while they fell over themselves in their blundering efforts to imitate her. This delighted them, and when she retired into the flat they would follow. The barrier I had erected in the doorway was high, but they constantly contrived to surmount it. After their occupation of the dining room the place had looked like a stable, and smelt like one; urine and excreta had soaked through all the protective layers of paper I had put down and glued them to the linoleum. Much work with a scrubbing brush and disinfectant was needed to restore the room to its original function. Now that the carpet was back they could not be readmitted. They could not be kept out.

Miss Canvey had impressed upon me that they must continue my guests for at least eight weeks, until they were weaned. I was not anxious to detain them for a moment longer, and had been canvassing their charms throughout the district ever since they were born. Miss

Canvey also said that I could get two or three pounds apiece for them; but I was not in need of money and thought I should be rid of them quicker if I gave them away. This may have been true, but it was mistaken policy for another reason, I fear, for people are apt to accept gifts too readily and value them less than purchases. At any rate I soon had a list of a dozen applicants for free puppies and, though I made few promises, considered the future secure. Tulip's local fame had helped me. She was well known and much admired. So eager, indeed, were some of my applicants to possess the offspring of so faithful and intelligent a bitch that, although they knew them to be mongrels, they quite pestered me for them, calling round at the flat from week to week to remind me of their claims. Any child of hers, they said, must surely be as wonderful as she.

Such flattering enthusiasm naturally disposed me kindly toward these petitioners. But before the gruelling eight weeks had dragged themselves out, something else had happened: I had developed a conscience. Much as I longed to be rid of the puppies, my feelings had become involved with them all individually, even, indeed particularly, with the two naughty little bitches, and as I watched upon my terrace the unfolding of these affectionate, helpless lives, and saw them adventuring, in ever-widening circles, into a life which they clearly thought positively smashing, my sense of responsibility towards them increased and became a discomfort to me. To 'find them homes,' as I had phrased it to myself, began to seem a totally inadequate description of my duty. I perceived that their whole future, their health and happiness, depended entirely upon me. Their lives were in my hands.

119

Many of my applicants were working-class people; my ambitions rose to a higher aim. Money, time, physical energy: Tulip's upkeep cost me all these in considerable quantities, and although I was not foolish enough to suppose that they constituted in themselves a guarantee of canine happiness, they might be thought to lay a hopeful foundation for it. They were none of them, it seemed to me, properties that the working classes had to spare or to speak of. Mental energy too: if I had learnt anything of dogs during my life with Tulip, it was that little is known about them, and I was always persevering after practical information. That little is known about them is not surprising; it is only within living memory that veterinary attention—previously confined to horses, cows and sheep—has been turned towards them. The homely, and often hair-raising, witchcraft that preceded their scientific study is still cherished in many an obstinate, uneducated mind. Even, in the beginning, I was mortified to find, in my own. One of the first things I recollected when I took charge of Tulip was that the family dogs, in my boyhood days, had always had a stick of sulphur in their drinking bowls. A prime necessity, of course. I hurried out and bought one. After it had been submerged in Tulip's bowl for a year it took on a grubby look and I decided to renew it. 'What do you want it for?' asked the chandler to whom I applied. Surprised by his ignorance, I explained. 'Have it by all means,' said he, 'but since sulphur is insoluble in water you could spend your money in better ways.'

Then there were many people who seemed to regard the dog as a purely utilitarian object, a protector for the home or a plaything for the kids. I had by now acquired a lively respect for canine qualities of heart and head, and did not wish to condemn Tulip's children to either of these fates. And the love of adolescent girls, whose virginal wombs maternally throb at the sight of a puppy, with which they grow quickly bored when it is puppy no more: that was another pitfall I intended to avoid. I therefore hoped to put the creatures out among adult, educated and prosperous people who had a personal feeling for dogs and the kind of lives they like to lead, a reasonable knowledge of their care and premises suitable for keeping them. But my hopes were not realized. I had a number of such persons on my list, two of whom, indeed, had already called and selected the puppies they wanted; but on various excuses they all let me down, and at a late hour when I could no longer wait to prosecute my search. For my landlord had intervened; someone in my block of flats, understandably disturbed by Tulip's parental agitations, had reported my activities; I had been told to get my animals, or myself, out of the place at once. In the event, my conditions, such as they were, had to be abandoned; the puppies went one by one to whomsoever would take them, after an only perfunctory investigation of the recipients' views and circumstances, or none at all.

How well did I do for them? The considerate question has now a specious look. How I did for them was of less urgency then than how I did for myself. That all the donees were kind people, of that I was confident, and that was the best for them that I did. It was much. It was little. For kindness is not enough, of course. Indeed, kindness can kill. Looking beyond their kindness I comforted myself with the reflection that since many of them were local residents I should be able to keep an eye on them and exercise, perhaps, some supervision over the welfare of their charges. All but one. Him, in my haste, I quite betrayed. For my list, which had once seemed so safe, ran out before the litter was wholly assigned, and I gave the last puppy to a shopkeeper friend who offered to find him a home. He was sold over the counter. To whom? I never discovered. What happened to him? I do not know.

In fact I did in the end what I had meant not to do, I cast them to fortune. It was, after all, I told myself, their inescapable fate. I had flown too high. They were mongrels and must take a mongrel's chance; in any case what assurance could there be that if I had done differently for them I should have done better? Health and happiness cannot be secured, and the only way to avoid the onus of responsibility for the lives of animals is never to traffic in them at all. Two of them died quite soon; one was run over in the dangerous road in which I had carelessly permitted him to live; the other developed 'fits' and was 'put to sleep.' I remember this latter specially well. She haunts me at times. She was the fattest and cosiest of the four bitches, always licking my hands and face with her tiny tongue in a quick responsive way. And she was the first to leave. Warm though the weather was, she shivered in my arms, I remember, as I carried her away from her brothers and sisters to the small Wandsworth council flat that was to be her future home. I placed her on the parlor table and she remained there, quite motionless except for the continual shivering, while the young female part of the family who were now her owners exclaimed how 'sweet' she was. She had a slight disfigurement, I recollect, a tiny cyst in the corner of one eye.

I saw her a number of times afterwards. She seemed

happy and devoted to her owners, they to her. A year
of life was all she had. Encountered one day without
her they told me she was dead, she had taken to having
'fits' and they had had her 'put to sleep.' She was perfectly all right otherwise, they admitted when I ques-
tioned them; in fact the vet had asked them why they
wished to destroy so healthy looking a young bitch; but
on account of the 'fits' they had insisted; they had
thought it kinder to her and best for everyone else to
have her 'put to sleep.' I did not trouble them further.
What was the use? I only wished they had consulted
me first. Dogs have 'fits' from all sorts of causes, mostly
ascertainable and remediable, often as simple as wrong-
feeding or worms, and need care and attention not sen-
tence of death. Tulip herself has occasional 'fits,' three
or four a year. Never satisfactorily diagnosed by the
many vets who have examined her and are necessarily
handicapped by not seeing her in the throes, they have
recurred now for so long, over a period of six years,
that I have come to regard them as idiosyncratic. She
loses the use of her hind legs and, temporarily para-
lysed, falls about the flat, or crouches, taut and trembling, with her fore-paws clenched, dribbling from the
mouth. Distressing to watch, these cramps or seizures
last, at most, for only half an hour and leave her with
no ill-effect at all; while she is 'suffering' (dogs make
a lot of fuss about nothing) she likes to be kissed and
fondled. Warm compresses beneath the tail seem also
to afford her pleasure if not relief; they were recommended by a vet who diagnosed an anal spasm. But
people are often frightened of their pets, and 'fits' excite
only panic fear; the spectre of rabies rears its ugly, and
long obsolete, head; the wife or kids may get bitten, and

the unfortunate animal is forthwith 'put to sleep'—a hypocritical euphemism that always disgusts me.

Of the rest of Tulip's progeny three were presently handed on, sold perhaps, by applicants who had begged most earnestly for them. I never saw them more. The impulse to follow up their small destinies soon weakened. Better not to know. The owner of one said it had been too difficult to house-train; the owner of another, an Irish laborer, spun a long story to account for its disappearance. Unable to keep it himself because it gnawed the legs of the furniture, he had given it to a friend in the Army. It was now the regimental mascot, beloved by all and having a wonderful time. I asked the name of the regiment. He became vague. In any case it had gone overseas, he said. It may have been true, and the animal had been his to dispose of as he wished: but how he had begged for it! A feeling of sickness overcame me. The place was poky, poor and full of children, no place for a dog, let alone a large one, which all Tulip's puppies promised to be, and it was, of course, a measure of the improvidence of the tenant, as of so many other people into whose hands I, no less improvidently, committed these animal lives, that he should particularly have wanted a large dog, a dog like Tulip, when he had not the circumstances to keep one—and could not even wait for it to grow. But perhaps the little creature had died, trodden on by one of his numerous children, and he was unwilling to admit it.

The remaining two, both bitches, stayed in Putney to grow up within a stone's throw of my flat and each other. Yet they were fated never again to meet. One of them I myself saw only once in all the years that followed, and that was when I called to enquire how she did. She inhabited a dark basement flat with a small backyard; the flat and the yard may be said to have composed her world. Her young owner, his sister and crippled father doted upon her, of course, but owing to the nature of their employment and the inflexibility of their social custom it was inconvenient for them to take her out until late in the evening when, at summer sun-down or in winter darkness, she rambled the streets for half-an-hour or so on the lead. It was not incon-venient for her young owner to have a Sunday mid-day pint in a pub I myself visited, but he never had his bitch with him. I always had mine. He gave of his animal always the cheerfulest accounts; it was only rather bleak and uncanny never to see her too. Many a time I urged him to bring her there to meet her mother and me. But, though promising to do so, he did not. He belonged to that conventional Sunday-best type of working-class per-son who cannot bear to be seen even carrying a parcel or doing anything that might attract attention to himself. She was an affectionate, pretty creature, very timid, he said. Small wonder. Was she happy? I suppose she was happy. She had, after all, fulfilled a dog's most urgent need, she had managed to bestow her heart, and upon steady people whose dull, uneventful lives required the consolation of what she had to give. She was not mated. I doubt if she encountered many other dogs, they were probably indoors by the time she got out. So was I. In all my constant promenades in the district with Tulip at all hours of the day over the years we never met her once. Not once.

Very different was the fortune of the other bitch, one

of the naughty ones who used to plague me so. She became a proper street dog, a canine *gamine,* and I met her frequently. No doubt, like her neighboring sister, she seldom saw grass, except the sparse and sooty blades that push up here and there in our towns, for putting the freedom of a walk in a dog's way seemed to her busy owners more reasonable than taking it out themselves; but though rarely venturing far she got round and about, became quite a 'person' in her street, hobnobbed with other dogs and eventually had a family of her own. More than any of the others in Tulip's litter she was her father's child; he bequeathed her all he had, his long and mottled coat and his odd pale-blue eye. But Tulip stamped her image also upon each of her children, and gave even to this one her silvery legs, one upstanding ear and, upon the brown-eyed side, her recognizable and touching profile. The creature was a grotesque; but she was a darling, a slim, fawning, gushing bitch. She never forgot us. Sighting us from afar, she would come bounding lightly along in a gracious yet diffident way, her feathery tail between her legs, to welcome us into her mean street. In front of her mother, she would positively swoon, collapsing in the road at her feet and rolling over onto her back. But Tulip would have none of her. Did she even recognize her? I could not be sure. If she did, she regarded her and her public demonstrations with a severe and perhaps jealous disapproval, and would push past or skirt round her with a growl, the fur rising a little on her neck and rump. This charming ugly duckling survived four years. She had been out of condition for some time, a dietary deficiency disease, for her owners had stubbornly rejected my advice, until confirmed by a vet, to continue to feed her the raw meat on which she had been weaned; 'raw meat makes dogs savage,' they maintained. Then she had a growth in the throat, said to be cancer. At last she could not swallow even water and had to be destroyed.

Tulip went through her confinement without turning a hair, almost without losing one. Another bitch in my district, an Airedale, who was brought to bed at about the same time, shed most of the hair on her back and presented a wretched, moth-eaten appearance. But the only hair Tulip lost was a small round patch on the underside of her tail, near the root. This came away because for a couple of months after her delivery she exuded from the womb a sticky pink jelly in consider-able quantities (dismissed by Miss Canvey as a normal after-birth event). Besides dropping about on the car-pets, it matted up the hair on that part of her tail which came in contact with the vulva. By the time I was able to groom her again much soap-and-water was required to disperse the clot, and the stifled hair came away with it, leaving a bald patch. But it soon grew again; and then, with her coat as glossy as ever, her figure as slim and her ways as skittish, no one could have guessed that she had recently been the mother of eight. But *I* did not emerge from the experience so unscathed. A number of serious mental notes had been taken on the way, all adding up to the same conclusion: never again! Opinion, expert and inexpert, in the dog world fully supported this decision. It was good for a bitch—so spoke the general voice—to have one litter in her life, and one was enough. What was meant by 'good'* and whom was envisaged by 'enough' I could not discover; but it was an opinion that suited me now. I had done my duty by Tulip; I had enabled her to have the full life it had always been my intention to give her; she had experienced sex and utilized her creative organs and maternal instincts; I need never have all that worry and trouble again.

* In his recent book *Marriage*, Mr. Kenneth Walker writes: 'There is no evidence that physical harm results from sexual continence. If any injury is inflicted by chastity, it is not on the body but on the mind.' Does this statement have any application to the lower animals?

6 · The Turn of the Screw

Tulip stands beside me on the upper deck of a 93 bus. She made her debut as a passenger of London Transport during the events related, and all our troubles—or so I hoped—were at an end. The bus is almost empty and we are right up in front. She is standing in the attitude she customarily adopts, her back to the engine, her fore-paws on the seat, her rump pressed up against the prow. She chose this position; it steadies her, and she appears also to derive a pleasurable kind of vibrant massage up her spine from the throbbing and quaking of the vehicle. Every now and then I see a small bead of blood trickle slowly and stainlessly down the white underside of her drooped tail and fall to the floor. This manifestation of her condition I conceal from the conductor. He seems a decent chap who would not mind; on the contrary he might be outraged and order us off. It is not a situation in which the English are notoriously quick with sympathy. And we must not offend him on any account. The time of his bus suits me; he was good enough to accept an Alsatian as passenger when I made preliminary inquiries a week ago; we have been travelling regularly with him since, and wish to go on doing so while his spell of duty lasts. For London bus conductors have turned out to be a powerful and capricious race. They can refuse to carry dogs and often do, even when their buses are empty and likely to remain so. 'Sorry, no dogs,' they say. Or, 'Only little dogs.' Or, less subtly, 'Too big.' Or, 'I've got one up there already, gov.,' as though two dogs could not conceivably be expected to meet without flying at each other's throats. Or (more frequently and crushingly), 'Not them dogs! Any dogs but them!' A few make no reply at all to my polite 'Will you carry her?' but, sparing me a tired look, press a firm thumb to the bell. So we are grateful to and dependent upon our present conductor and do not wish to try his indulgence too far by letting him see the tiny trackless rubies run from long white hair to long white hair down the droop of Tulip's tail.

It is 6:45 A.M., and we are on our way to Wimbledon Common. If these various facts are put together the importance of our bus becomes plain. The Putney dogs are still abed, so we have reached it without molestation. To be sure, the stop is only some five hundred yards from my flat; but I have been developing an elaborate plan of campaign, and two considerations have influenced it at this point. It would never do to reach the stop in a fracas of dogs; the conductor might twig our trouble and change his mind. Also I do not want Tulip physically or emotionally upset. I want her to get through her season as peacefully as possible. And as pleasantly. Let other bitches in her condition be punished—for so it must seem to them—by being imprisoned for three weeks, *she* shall lose nothing. Now that we have the co-operation of London Transport, she shall have just as happy a time as she normally has. Indeed, I will fix it for her so naturally, there will be so little apparent difference in her way of life, that she will scarcely know she is in heat at all. Exertion will be required on my side. I am perfectly ready to expend it. I am anxious to expend it. I wish her to have a wonderful time. I wish her to have absolutely everything she wants. . . .

So it is 6:45 on a summer's morning. I am unwashed and unshaven. Some tea is in my stomach. We have not crossed the front doorstep of our block of flats. Dogs will not therefore congregate there and annoy the porter and the other tenants by urinating in the vestibule as they used to do. A cellar window which I have discovered at the rear of the building has given us egress. Through it we have emerged, morning after morning, always at precisely the same time, Tulip running free. Except for the unusual earliness of the hour and the oddity of our means of exit, there has been nothing to discompose her, nothing to suggest to her mind the exceptional, and therefore perhaps the deceitful. If she has been surprised, as sometimes, in the searching look up and down the road she at once casts, she appears to be, at the persistent doglessness of the landscape—for she is now, of course, particularly drawn to her own kind—will not this have seemed to her more the merest bad luck than anything to be blamed upon me? And whatever momentary disappointment she may have suffered, has it not been instantly stifled by anticipation of the joys that lie ahead?

We are safe. We are free. The bus trundles up Putney High Street and stops alongside No. 2. The Pines, where Swinburne lived. Up Putney Hill it goes, and now we are running by the edge of the Common. We can dismount anywhere here, but there are some points better avoided—rangers' cottages and their dogs—and in time I know all the safest tracks. Once over the road we are among trees and bracken, lost to the world of dogs and of men. Crossing the open plateau with its golf course, we give a wide berth to the Windmill, where Lord Cardigan fought his duel in 1840, where Lord Baden-Powell wrote part of his *Scouting for Boys* in 1908, and descend into the birch woods on the far slopes.

This is our goal, our haven. Here, where the silver trees rise in their thousands from a rolling sea of bracken, Tulip turns into the wild beast she resembles. Especially at this early hour the beautiful, remote place must reek of its small denizens, and the scent of the recent passage of rabbits and squirrels, or the sound of the nervous beating of their nearby hidden hearts, throws her into a fever of excitement. The bracken is shoulder high, but soon she is leaping over it. Round and round she goes, rhythmically rising and falling, like a little painted horse in a roundabout, her fore-legs flexed for pouncing, her tall ears pricked and focused, for she has located a rabbit in a bush. Useless to go straight in after it, she has learnt that; the rabbit simply dives out the other side and is lost. Her new technique is cleverer and more strenuous. She must be everywhere at once. She must engirdle the crafty, timid creature and confuse it with her swiftness so that it knows not which way to turn. And barking is unwisdom, she has discovered that too, for although it may add to the general terrorizing effect of her tactic, it also hinders her own hearing of the tiny, furtive movement in the midst of the bush. Silently, therefore, or with only a muted whimpering of emotion, she rises and falls, effortlessly falls and rises, like a dolphin out of the green sea among the silver masts, herself the color of their bark, battling her wits with those of her prey. The rabbit can bear no more and makes its dart; in a flash, with a yelp, she is after it, streaking down the narrow track. Rabbits are agile and clever. This one flies, bounds, doubles, then bounces like a ball and shoots off at right angles. But Tulip is clever too. She knows now where the burrows lie and is not to be hoodwinked. The rabbit has fled downhill to the right; she sheers off to the left, and a tiny scream pierces the quiet morning and my heart. Alas, Tulip has killed! I push through the undergrowth to the scene of death. She is recumbent, at breakfast. Casting an anxious glance over her shoulder at my approach, she gets up and removes her bag to a safer distance. I follow. She rises again, the limp thing in her jaws, and confronts me defiantly. How pretty is her wilful face! It is a young rabbit. Shall I take it from her? I can if I wish. She will yield it up, reluctantly but without rancor. Tapeworms and coccidia lurk in rabbits' livers and intestines. Never mind, let her keep it; it is a well-earned prize, and now, particularly, she must have everything she wants . . .

Seating myself on a fallen tree I light a cigarette. She sits too, and addresses herself once more to her meal. I hear the crunch of the tender bones and the skull, bone still warm with the lust of the young creature's life. She devours it all, fur, ears, feet; not a trace of her banquet remains. Now she knows she is both thirsty and hot and, with her loping stride, leads me down to the nearest stream and flops into it. Reclining on one flank she laps the shallow water, letting her long tail float out upon the surface: she is momentarily conscious of her condition and is cooling her swollen vulva, her nipples and her anus. Fern drapes the banks of the pool she has chosen, the early sun slants across her through the branches of a mountain ash, the water sings over its pebbly bed: it is Africa and she is a jungle beast come down to the river to bathe. From one flank to the other she shifts; delicious the cool stream flowing about her heated parts; when she emerges she will not shake herself, she has learnt that also, to keep the refreshing liquid clinging about her; she will be hot and dry again soon enough . . .

It is summer, it is spring . . . I keep her out two hours, three hours, four hours . . . She is on the go all the time. Can nothing tire her sufficiently? Ah, would that I could keep her here for ever, so happy and so

free . . . The journey back presents no difficulties. The
85 bus from the top of Roehampton Lane suits us now.
We may have to wait about for an agreeable conductor,
but the stop is countrified, no dogs will harass us here.
The bus drops us at Putney Bridge, from where we set
out. We still have that five hundred yards to walk home
and must expect, at this late morning hour, to encounter
a dog or two who will notice and follow her; but now
it does not matter—I have worked it all out—she is exhausted, she is muddy and wet, the streams will have
washed away the potent emanations of yesterday. Soon
we are through the cellar window and back in the flat.
I dry her and give her some milk, warm if the weather
is cold. Then I shave and wash, make myself some coffee
and set off for work. Tulip is curled up contentedly in
my armchair when I go in to bid good-bye to her.

'Ah, Tulip,' I say, 'what a lucky girl you are! What
other bitch in your condition has so wonderful a time?
Now rest till tomorrow morning, when we will do it all
over again . . .'

But Nature will not be cheated, fooled, bribed, fobbed
off, shuffled out of the way. I still have to return in the
evening, and, dodge it as I may, I know what I shall
find, a burning creature burning with desire. 'Heat' is the
apt word; one can feel against one's hand without touching her the feverous radiations from her womb. A fire
has been kindled in it, and no substitute pleasure can
distract, no palliative soothe, no exertion tire, no cooling stream slake, for long the all-consuming need of her
body. She is enslaved. She is possessed. Indeed, especially towards the peak—it is the strangest, the most
pitiful thing—her very character is altered. This independent, unapproachable, dignified and single-hearted

creature, my devoted bitch, becomes the meekest of beg-
gars. Anyone will do who will supply her with a crumb
of physical comfort. Some years later I take her with
me everywhere in this condition, and in the quiet public
house restaurant where I often eat my lunch, she will
go from table to table looking not for food but for love.
Leaning her flank against the knees of the other cus-
tomers, she gazes up at them with humble eyes. People
are often flattered when animals seem to select them for
affection, and women especially will exclaim with pleasure when Tulip behaves like this. If they know her
already they will exclaim with surprise: 'Why, look at
Tulip! What's come over you, dear? I never knew you
so friendly before.' Nor, in a few days, will they know
her so friendly again, unless they happen upon her six
months hence. But now she is a poor beggar cast upon
the mercy of the world. They stroke her. If they stroke
her head, that is not what she wants; she will shift herself further round to present them with her rump, and
stand there meekly, with lowered head, while their hands
move over it. When they stop, she will thank them with
a grateful look and push it at them again. Human beings
are extraordinarily ignorant about dogs. These amused
and flattered people do not notice the coiling tail; if they
noticed it they would not know what it meant; if they
knew what it meant they would probably be less flattered
and amused.

It is what I myself have to face when I return. I have
had it all before, of course, as readers of this history
may exclaim: but with what a difference! Then I was
working to help her; now I am bent upon frustrating her.
If I saw her state at all then as a plight, I could contem-
plate it with equanimity, with cheerfulness; I cannot

bear it now. I cannot bear it, I cannot avoid it, she ob-
trudes it constantly upon my sight. 'Help me,' she says,
gazing at me with her confident animal eyes; but I no
longer wish to help her, I wish to frustrate her, I wish
her to have everything in the world she wants, except
the thing she needs. She presses up against me. I put
down my hand and stroke her, her soft ears, her pretty
head, her backbone, her coiling tail. The tail is sign
enough of her physical torment. So rigid is it that a
small effort is required to disengage it from the flank
to which it clings. When I draw it through my hand it
recoils upon her body like a steel spring, and whips,
as though imbued with a life of its own, from side to
side. How cruel a trick, I think, to concentrate, like a
furnace, the whole of a creature's sexual desire into
three or four weeks a year. Yet is she worse or better
off than ourselves who seek gratification of it, without
respite, over the greater part of our lives? She rises up
and clasps my leg.

'Ah, Tulip, you know you didn't like it last time.
Don't you remember how frightened you were? And
those poor children of yours, how bored you got with
them!'

But Nature has her in thrall:

'You shall mate! You shall bear! And now! Now!
My time is short and must not be wasted!'

'Help me,' she says, pressing against me, staring up
into my face, bringing me her trouble. I cannot bear it.
With a rough word I send her from me. She goes, de-
jected, rebuffed (dogs are expert at inflicting remorse),
and sits on the bed at the other side of the room facing
me. Unendurable the hopeful gaze watching for signs
of relentment, the sorry sighs she heaves. A smile would

bring her over, even a look. I avert my face. But she cannot rest. Nature will not let her rest. Soon she has slid off the bed, and by a halting, circuitous route, reached me again to replace herself in my line of vision. The tall ears are erect now, the head drawn back, the gaze level. I meet it, in spite of myself. We stare into each other's eyes. The look in hers disconcerts me, it contains too much, more than a beast may give, something too clear and too near, too entire, too dignified and direct, a steadier look than my own. I avert my face. Raising a paw she bangs me on the knee.

'No, Tulip.'

But delicately finding room for her fore-feet on the seat of my chair, she rises up towards me and sets her cheek to mine . . . Darkness, which quickly extinguishes canine activity, is slow to affect her now. I go to bed early to end the dismal day, but she is instantly beside me, sitting upright against my pillow, her back turned, shifting, licking, panting, shifting, peering at my face, pulling at my arm. Sweet creature, what am I doing to you? I stretch out my hand in the gloom and stroke the small nipples which, I have decided, shall never again fulfil their natural purpose. Panting, she slackly sits while my hand caresses her, her ears flattened, her head dropped, gazing with vacant eyes into the night beyond the windows. Gradually she relaxes, subsides. Gradually, my hand upon her, she sleeps . . .

How do other people cope? All bitch-owners must have the same problem, though the luckier ones have it less frequently. Tulip is fairly normal and regular, a six- or seven-month bitch, but there are many deviations; some bitches are quite erratic and unpredictable, some have only one heat a year, and I am told of one who lived healthily to the age of thirteen without ever coming into heat at all. Fortunate owner! For some reason Nature missed her out. No doubt, too, the degree of intensity varies from breed to breed, from bitch to bitch, but every private owner must have the same problem in some sort, and I ask about. The answers come readily enough. 'Send her to kennels. That's what we always do.' 'Haven't you a spare room to shut her up in?' 'Have her altered.' And then the voice I most fear and detest: 'Kick her out of the way, the dirty bitch!'

I listen, but I cannot act. How can I put her from me? Situated as I am, I see that I never should have taken her at all; I cannot mend that now. She is my friend, an honored member of my household. Years of devotion, years of habit, bind us together. When she is hurt, it is to me that she comes, holding out her paw. When she goes home it is into my door that she turns. It is true that she is now more amiable to strangers than is her wont, but as I think of that I remember also her desperate, her frenzied agitation whenever she loses sight of me in the streets. I cannot send her from me. And how can I tamper with so beautiful a beast? Yet I *am* tampering with her. I am frustrating her.

A few people who adopt none of these measures but get their animals, somehow or other, through their difficulties as I do, say: 'Luckily it doesn't last long. It's soon over.' Soon! Will the wretched season never drag itself out? And even when it seems safely past, its ghost rises accusingly from the grave. Two months later, when she could have been having a litter, she thinks she is pregnant. Her lower teats begin to secrete milk. She moves restlessly about the flat choosing her place, making her plans. Lying awake in the night I hear her, sometimes in the bathroom, the smallest, darkest room in the flat, scratching away at the linoleum; sometimes out on the terrace, mysteriously prowling among the weathered ruins of her old box, scratching, scratching at the decaying wood, making a nest for children that will never be born . . . Soon it will be over. The ghost rises. Soon it will start again . . . Must I have this recurrent nightmare forever? Do bitches have change of life? It seems they do not. And is it my imagination that the more I frustrate her the more protracted, the more insistent, her heats become? As though Nature were saying: 'You escaped me last time. You shall not escape me this!'

It is spring, it is winter, it is summer . . . Through twilight darkness, through the rain, through sunshine, frost, or heavy dew, I make my way with her across the plateau to the birch woods to give her everything she wants, except the thing she needs. She is four, she is five, she is six . . . Spots of blood on the silvery shins. The torment, the wonder, has begun again. Like a flower, like a door, the vagina is opening, the house is being made ready, the peremptory, the remorseless summons approaches . . . It is her tenth day, her eleventh day, her twelfth day. Soon it will be over. Only two days more. Only two days more before desire fails, fecundity fails—opportunity fails. Soon the flower will close, the door will shut, will lock; we shall be free, we shall be safe . . . How beautiful she is in her shining raiment, her birch-bark body, her sable bodice, her white cravat, her goffered ruff. Exquisite the markings on her face, her turning, turning face, like the wing of a Marbled

White butterfly. Perfection of form. Perfection of grace. My burning bitch, burning in her beauty and her heat . . .

'Well, Tulip, I promise you, if ever you meet an Alsatian dog as handsome as yourself, alone and palely loitering in the woods, that will be romance, that will be fate, and I won't stand in your way.'

A safe bet! That very season we meet one and in those circumstances, a noble beast who has probably scented her while out walking with his owners, for the woods must be impregnated with her sexual odor, and returned alone to seek her. She goes to welcome him, her sharp face sharpened with mischief. They savor each other, their noses, their bodies; their uplifted tails wave graciously like plumes. Over her shoulder she turns upon me a gay, inclusive, conspiratorial look. They begin to play. He advances eagerly upon her, trampling with his feet. She retreats, curtsying down, gazing up shrewdly into his face. He presses forward. She fends him off, leaping backwards, switching her bottom from side to side as he tries to approach it, first by one flank, then by the other. They rise up together breast to breast, clasping each other in their arms. They are like two boxers amicably sparring, leading, feinting, guarding, trying for the advantage. He presses on. She turns and flees, her ears laid back. He flies after. How enchanting she is, the coquettish little bitch, putting forth all her bitchiness. Now she halts. She is still. She stands. He mounts her. And before I know that I have spoken, her name is out of my mouth. 'Tulip!' With her bright attentive face she comes to me at once. I put her on the lead and take her home. I am profoundly shocked, profoundly shaken. Life has caught me out, and the word that I have uttered rings on and on in my head. The dog does not molest us, nor does he ever cross our path again . . .

It is autumn, it is spring . . . The birch woods, and she is off upon her errands, I upon mine. The solitary place belongs to us. It is our private garden, our temple, our ivory tower. Except for an occasional ranger or woodman we seldom meet a soul. I make my way towards the tree upon which, yesterday, I left my cap. The illusion of happiness, of peace, must have continuity, must have permanence. Moving up between the thin silver pillars that line the way to the second crest, I look down into the grove where, in isolated grandeur, the great birch tree stands. Lord of the woods, like a giant buried upside down to the waist, his huge open legs, green at the thighs, tower sprawling into the air. The narrow track, hedged with high bracken, passes between them over his crotch. It is the heart of the woods, the sacred precinct, and with Tulip beside me I descend into it. The place belongs to us. I know many of its secrets now, many of its joys and sorrows. Tulip is adding to the latter; I regret it, but love is cruel. It pleases her to chase and kill; she must have her pleasure. She must have everything she wants, except the thing she needs. While she persecutes, I protect; thus may I balance the accounts, perhaps, hers and mine, and propitiate the tutelary god. It is spring, and I visit the nesting birds upon whose private affairs we have stumbled. The mallard has built too close to the track; how can she hope to escape detection? When Tulip's rummagings disturbed her, what valor she displayed, feigning injury beneath our very feet to lure us from her eggs. Fortunately for her, Tulip is not interested in birds. They have outsmarted her too often. While the mallard's oriental eye watches me from her prickly bower, I draw the long arms of the bramble more thickly about her and screen her from view. Later on, perhaps, we shall see her leading her brood down to Queensmere. Or we shall not. We may find a cold and rifled nest . . .

'You could destroy the litter . . .'

'Could you?'

'I think so.'

'Life is tenacious. They die hard.'

'Yes.'

'Why are you changing your mind, anyway?'

'I don't know. She is so pretty.'

'So you would destroy her pretty babies?'

'Not all. I would leave her two to draw off her milk.'

'Three. One of two might die, leaving only one.'

'Then three.'

'Four would be safer.'

'Then four.'

'Ha-ha! You amuse me. And how would you abstract the rest?'

'I keep trying to think . . .'

'She would know. Close all the doors between, her tall ears would hear the little shrieks!'

'Don't! It's what I dread.'

'Poor fellow! But please explain: what has her prettiness to do with it?'

'It will be lost.'

'What is that to you? Or to her? Unless, as I suspect, you want one of her babies for yourself to carry on when she is dead?'

'Oh no! Not all this responsibility again! I don't think I could.'

'You don't think! Would it not be true to say that you are woefully lacking in decision?'

'Woefully. It's the frustration really. I hate to see it.'

'Then you'll be mating her and destroying her litters every time she's in heat?'

'No, no! Just this once.'

'Every time you don't you'll have to see frustration.'

It is summer, and heath fires have broken out. The sultry air is acrid with the smell of burning. Inexorable fires that smolder away below the peaty soil, flickering up from time to time a momentary flower of flame as they gnaw their way towards the roots of the trees. Dear Willow, foremost ever with tidings of spring; my Sweet Chestnut, who lays down for me every autumn a carpet of the palest gold; how can I help you? I stamp and stamp along the devouring edge, puffs of ash spurt up beneath my feet. Out! Out! It is out . . . But when I glance back the wisps of death are rising once more.

'If they don't die of one thing they die of another,' the woodman says. 'Trees go sick, just like we do, they all have their diseases. Some go sick in the foot, some in the head. I can always tell a sick tree. They bleed too. The birch bleeds red, like us. See.' He thrusts his finger into a hole in the tree he is logging and brings out a thick orange slime. 'I won't ask you to smell it. When you're sawing up a birch and get a pocket of this under your nose it doesn't do to bend over it too long, it turns the stomach. It's a birch disease; you'll see it about if you look, a black mark ten foot or so up the stem and this stuff spilling out of it. A woodpecker started this one going, I reckon. He pecks and he pecks, and if he pecks a hole the rain can settle in, the tree goes bad inside.'

'Is he an enemy of yours, then?'

'The woodpecker? He has to live. We all have to live. He has his troubles like the rest of us. Oh no, I wouldn't care to speak against the birds. I like the birds and they like me. I've had them coming down to me many a time as I work. When there's snow on the ground I just clear it away with my foot, like this, and they dive in. They're grateful if you help them, and they help you in return. I'm on my own most of the time and they tell me when anyone's coming. They fly over to tell me. The squirrel he tells me too. Just like your dog tells you . . .'

It is winter. It is her thirteenth day. It was on her thirteenth day that she was fertilized, three years ago. Today she could be fertilized. Probably not tomorrow. Tomorrow may be too late. The door will close, will lock. Soon it will be over. Soon it will be too late . . . I pick up the broken glass that is everywhere to be found and upon which Tulip sometimes cuts her feet. I pick it up throughout the year wherever I notice it, but it is only now when the high summer seas of bracken have sunk to a low brown froth that I can see it where I fear it most, at their roots. Here, where she was so lately pouncing . . . The scattered fragments of broken bottle are bad enough—so sharp that, cautiously though I gather them, I often prick my fingers—but in their midst I sometimes find the butt-end still planted upright in the turf where boys stuck it, the other day or years ago, as a target for their stones. Its splintered sides stand up like spears. I gaze at Tulip's slender, long-toed feet in dismay. The little knuckly bones that curve over the four front pads are more delicate than a bird's claw. And the pads themselves: I used to suppose them made of some tough, resistant, durable substance, such as rubber or gutta-percha; but they are sponges of blood. The tiniest thorn can pierce them, a sharp edge of glass, trodden on merely at walking pace, can slice them open like grapes. How they bleed! And what an age they take, by slow granulation, to heal! Together they fit, indeed, to form a kind of quilted cushion; but dogs spread their toes for pouncing, and in between is only soft furry flesh and all the vital tendons of the leg. One pounce upon this bottle, with both front feet perhaps . . . I pick it up. I pick it all up, every tiny fragment. I seek it out, I root it up, this lurking threat to our security, our happiness, in the heart of the wood; day after day I uncover it and root it up, this disease in the heart of life. I dispose it where it can do least harm; I bury it at the foot of the trees, I cast it into the midst of the densest thorn or furze. But not into this holly thicket, for last year a man entered it to die. So deep did he burrow into his green unwelcoming shroud that it was many days before his body was found, his empty phial beside him. Not at the foot of this oak, with its curtsying stem and long proffered arm . . . Again the choice was made. Who made it? Carrying his rope with him from Kingston at night, he moved up through the dark woods, clambered here and dropped off into space. It gave the ranger who found him 'quite a turn' to see him standing there, his feet off the ground, so steady and so still. Who? Why? The failed, the frustrated lives pass on, leaving no trace. The place must be full of ghosts . . . And young Holland, where did he die? Where is the swamp into which he drove his face? Lost, lost, the inconsiderable, anguished deed in the blind hurry of time. The perfect boy face downwards in a swamp . . . The doctor who performed the autopsy remarked that the muscles and limbs were absolutely perfect, he had never seen a better developed boy in his life, nor, when he split open the skull, such deep gray matter. Ah, perfect but imperfect boy, brilliant at work, bored by games, traits of effeminacy were noticed in you, you were vain of your appearance and addicted to the use of scent. Everyone, it seemed, wished you different from what you were, so you came here at last and pushed your face into a swamp, and that was the end of you, perfect but imperfect boy . . .*

The cold night mists are still dissolving from the naked grove. The ground is brittle with frost. Out of their ragged green trousers the huge legs of the giant birch sprawl above my head. I pause for a moment upon his crotch and gaze fearfully upward. It looks no worse, the black mark and the thin trickle of blood, too high to reach, too high for my eyes at first to be sure, until I perceived the repulsive white fungi, like brackets, sprouting about it. He is sick, the great tree, he is doomed. It is a secret between us, but not for long will he escape the woodman's notice. They will cut off his legs, I think, as I pass between them prodding for glass. They will throw him down, the Lord of the Woods, I say to myself as I linger at the edge of the grove looking back. There is a sudden scurry of noise, and Tulip flies across the ride on which I stand, her nose to the ground. Out of the tattered undergrowth on one side, into the tattered undergrowth on the other, she rushes; she has come, she has gone, silence claps down again, it is as though she never had been. Excepting that, caught upon the cinders of the ride in front of me curls and wavers in the frozen air the warm white fume of her breath. I watch it as it clings, writhes, wavers, slowly dissolves. She has been, she has gone, nothing now remains. Soon it will be over. Soon it will be too late . . .

* *The Times:* June 30, 1926.

Appendix

'None of the dogs I see here ever has any sexual experience,' said a prominent and busy West-end vet to me
the other day. I was not surprised, though faintly shocked
to hear professionally stated a conclusion I had already
reached. 'Clients often ask me if I can't find wives for

their dogs, but (he shrugged) what can I do?' After a moment he added: 'Some breeds are sexier than others. Poodles and Airedales, for instance.'

It must, indeed, be clear enough from the foregoing pages that for the urban dog at any rate expectation of sex is slender in the extreme. He is equipped for it, but the equipment is not used. There is a human conspiracy against him—a conspiracy I could hardly fail to notice since I was taking part in it myself. Charitably disposed in my sense of security on Wimbledon Common, it was but another step from self-congratulation at having kept Tulip successfully out of his way to ask myself what, in that case, he did. Could the answer be anything but 'Nothing'? No doubt a grandee dog, of interest to the breeding industry, could gain occasional reentry for stud purposes into the kennel from which he emerged. But the thousands of other dogs, the less highly bred, the mongrels, what about them? Bitches, in any case, are far fewer than dogs; though thought to be more faithful, they are also more trouble and, increasingly now when the flat is superseding the private house, the problems they present are undesirable, if not impracticable. Small prospect, then, of the urban dog picking up stray females in the street; I and my fellow bitch-owners were taking care of that. And the smarter his postal address the fainter his hopes. In working-class areas, where greater laxity and muddlement prevail, his chances of self-help are somewhat better; but even a working-class dog must surely think himself singularly fortunate if once in the course of his life he happens upon a stray bitch, of accessible size, in heat and at a consenting moment of her heat, unanointed with 'Keep-away,' irradiated chlorophyll, eucalyptus oil, or some similarly repellent preparation, and unescorted by other and perhaps stronger dogs with whom he will have to dispute his claim. Even then the technical trial-and-error problem of intromission, increased by lack of practice, remains to be solved. Stray matings, of course, do occur; but when it is considered that the animals are then immobilized for half an hour or more and can scarcely be expected to have exercised much tact in their choice of a suitable site, if any choice exists, the fact that one seldom sees dogs copulating in the streets might seem circumstantial evidence of the rarity of the event. If seen, human intervention, never far off and now in the shape of a bucket of water, is likely to put to hard-won success a premature end. I have twice seen the application of this curious remedy for canine sex, and—let us be charitable—its employment may sometimes be due to ignorance. An intelligent retired police-sergeant told me that he himself had always supposed it to be 'helpful,' an act of kindliness. When two dogs were found 'stuck together' in the street, something, he thought, had 'gone wrong,' human aid was needed to get them out of their difficulty, the bucket of water was the prescribed, the efficacious, thing. It is necessary to add that he disliked dogs and had not therefore troubled to acquaint himself with their problems. But hatred too—the Abbé Tolbiac—lends impulse to the douching hand; the possible rupturing of the bitch by having shocked out of her the instrument which Nature has purposely constructed to remain indefinitely locked within is of small concern to the outraged puritan mind prating of public decency and the corruption of the young. Whether country dogs fare better in this matter I do not know.

.   .   .

All that remains for the town dog then is that his owners will buy him a wife or fix up something for him by private introduction. Excepting where a little side-line breeding for profit is the motive, the likelihood of either troublous course being pursued is small. Out of curiosity merely, as I go about in the dog world, I pop my question: 'Has he ever been married?' The answer is usually no. There is often good-will; the obstacles are too great. Some people, generally the owners of breed dogs, claim to have tried and failed: 'Matter of fact I did find him a bitch once, but he wouldn't look at her'— or 'she wouldn't look at him.' Bitches, to whom also I apply my question, naturally come off rather better, at any rate when pedigree; they have their establishments if litters are required; but in their case too the answer is often no. Some people believe they hate sex; others regard it as unnecessary, or odious, or positively dangerous. Some, hugging to themselves all the love, which dogs feel only for the human race, will not allow that there is a sexual instinct also. To this large category belong those nervous women who, far from being sympathetic to intimate canine relationships, prevent their creatures, male or female, even from speaking to their own kind. Never off the lead, they are twitched away from all communication with other dogs, in case of fights, contagion, or 'nasty' behavior, they are so greatly loved. Men, too, frequently exhibit the deepest aversion to such poor sexual satisfactions as are left to their beasts. I meet it constantly, the intolerant reaction to the natural conduct of a dog and a bitch. No sooner does some canine admirer begin to pay Tulip court than the master's stick will stir, the reproof will be uttered: 'Come off it, Rex! Now stop it, I say! How often must I tell you?' Nor can 'the feelings of others,' though they may occasionally be the modest motive, always be advanced in excuse, for the same thing happens when there is no one else about. 'Do let them be!' I sometimes expostulate. 'They're doing no harm.' But the stick stirs. One gentleman, fidgeting from foot to foot in the solitude of Putney Common, exclaimed: 'I *hate* to see dogs do that!'

When Tulip is actually in the canine news—that is to say when she is on the verge of heat or just coming out of it—incidents are more frequent and more serious. The little dog approaches her and begins to flatter her. This she graciously permits. The master, who is stationary ten paces away watching the rowing crews on the river, notices and calls his dog. Both animals are safely on the sidewalk, they are clearly on the best of terms, the master is in no hurry. But the amount of totally unnecessary interference in canine lives, the exercise of authority for its own sake, has to be seen to be believed. The little creature cannot tear himself away. The master calls more harshly. The dog wags his tail but cannot go. Sensing trouble, I summon Tulip and put her on the lead.

'It's not his fault,' I say mildly. 'I'm afraid my bitch is just coming into heat.'

The master gives me a brief look but no reply. He calls a third time, and now that Tulip has been withdrawn, the little dog rejoins him, wagging his tail.

'Come here!' says the master, the lead dangling from his hand.

The little dog approaches, very humble, very apologetic, looking winningly up into his face. What he sees does not reassure him. He comes to a nervous halt.

'Come here!' says the master, upright in his Aquascutum.

The little dog creeps forward to his very feet. The master lashes out. With a yelp the little dog shrinks away.

'Come here!' says the master.

Inch by inch, on his stomach, the little dog crawls once more up to his master's boots. The lash descends. Now the master is satisfied. A lesson has been taught. Two lessons, one lash for each: obedience, propriety. He squares his shoulders and their interrupted walk is resumed.

But in all my questionings about the sexual lives of dogs, I have never met anyone else who deliberately threw, as I did, a pedigree bitch to a mongrel—though I have met a few pedigree bitches who managed to throw themselves to mongrels and got families thereby. The trial-and-error stories I hear, from which after one failure, owners draw the perhaps convenient conclusion that since bitch refused dog or dog refused bitch, dog or bitch does not really like sex at all, are always intrabreed matches. The inference may be true; but I often wonder nevertheless whether the result would have been the same if the animals had been allowed to choose for themselves. A woman biologist, when told that Tulip had appeared to prefer a mongrel sire, remarked: 'Shows her good sense.'*

I had not failed to notice, from the beginning of this history, the alacrity with which dog-owners responded to

* The working classes still cling to the superstition, long ago discredited, that a pedigree bitch is ruined by sexual promiscuity and can never afterwards have a pure litter.

my pimping propositions. None of them required a fee, none of them wanted that other recognized due for sire-service, the first pick of the litter; they simply wanted their dogs to copulate, and they were remarkably eager to secure this result. Such keenness, together with the vet's statement quoted above, might be taken as evidence of conscience, of a humane concern for a dog's needs and welfare. This is often the sincere motive. But I fancy that less disinterested considerations sometimes complicate it. I have said earlier that the bitch is more trouble than the dog. Is it true? By trouble is meant, of course, sexual trouble. That the bitch is certainly a trouble when she is in heat will not be disputed by readers of these pages; but she is in heat for, at most, six weeks in the year. For ten and a half months she might be said to be absolutely sexless. In a dog, on the other hand, and particularly in certain breeds of dog, sexual discomfort is liable to obtrude itself at any time. He is then an embarrassment to the ladies and a source of inconvenient wonder to the children. It is difficult to know what to do with the poor fellow except kick him under the table or turn him out of the room. Nor is that all. Fear enters. Fear of pets is far more prevalent than is realized; the larger the pet the greater the fear. May the animal not go 'funny' through frustration? Perhaps he does.

All these factors—embarrassment, fear, snobbery—came curiously together once in my own experience. The years of worry and distress described in the last chapter gradually wore my resolution down; I began to revolve plans for mating Tulip again. Could I not find some local side-line Alsatian breeder who would not only mate her but house her while she whelped and suckled? The litter should be his, I would also pay board and lodging and visit her daily.

One day I observed in the street a young working man with a pretty male Alsatian so similar to Tulip in color and marking that, although I had been told that one could not breed for color, 'made for each other' was the thought that sprang to my mind. I accosted the owner and got the usual eager response. He was not merely willing, he was actually on the look-out for the very thing that I proposed. Later on I visited him. But either he had misunderstood or misled me: botheration over litters was no part of his plan. All he wanted was sex for his dog, and he wanted that badly. He, his wife and sister were at work all day; the dog was left behind for long hours to guard the small council house in which they lived. A friendly creature, no doubt he grew lonely. Dogs love company. They place it first in their short list of needs. This great wolf-like beast was so emotionally over-wrought when his human friends returned that he went quite mad with excitement and exhibited then and for the rest of the evening an unbecoming eroticism that deeply disturbed them, the more so since they were the objects of it. I take this to be a commonplace in canine-human relationships. Knowing nothing, in spite of constant efforts to inform them, of the Expulsion from Eden, dogs remain lamentably innocent and uninhibited in their emotions; worse, they are all too liable to confuse sex and pleasure and, having no outlet for the former, to address the whole boiling to their beloved owners. Tulip herself, when I offer her some delicious prospect such as an unexpected walk, will often try to rape me as we go down in the elevator, a demonstration of gratitude

I should regard myself as churlish to rebuff. But normally such behavior is ill-received and checked. This young man was both ashamed and alarmed by his dog's love. A bitch, he thought, might cool his ardor off.

When I got up to go, I noticed through his window a large concourse of dogs on the far side of the road and commented idly upon the number his district seemed to contain. He said angrily:

'Yes, there's a rotten old cow lives over there with a dirty bitch, and she's always letting her roam about loose when she's on heat to upset the dogs. I've reported her to the police once, and I've a jolly good mind to do so again.'

'But isn't that the very thing you want?' I asked with surprise. 'Why not let your own dog out to have a go at her?'

'What, with *that* thing!' he exclaimed with indescribable scorn.

With the failure of these new plans for mating Tulip, the end of the long journey was at last in view. The interminability of her heats when I was frustrating her, the urgency of the fleeting moment when I was trying to serve her, I could bear neither of them any more. I had interfered too much in her life already. I would interfere no longer. I would neither hinder nor assist. I wanted no further authority in her personal affairs. Whatever the consequences might be she must have *carte blanche*. She must take her chances, suit herself. She must go free. . . . But safety first: in order that she should not be douched and ruptured, other dogs should not be whipped, I should not be fined for allowing her to copulate in public, and the English race should not be affronted, *carte blanche* had to be modified: time, place, and the loved one must come together. Time now could be any time, place should be reasonably private and would have to be reached, the loved one must be left to luck. In her eighth year then I set forth with her in her seasons on this path of qualified freedom. And now everything was easy, life, mind, she made it so. She was, after all, by designation, a sheep dog, with some special aptitude for taking charge; as soon as I gave her leave to take it I saw that I need never have troubled myself at all. Trotting along beside me, her bright loving gaze constantly on my face, she read unerringly my wishes. Importunate dogs molesting her in public had to be put in their place; at a sign from me she put them there. Wrinkling up her black lips and clashing her crocodile jaws, she flew at them with a fine pretence of vexation. They rebounded of course, for they understood her perfectly; when the offence was repeated she scattered them again. It was, indeed, the very thing she had tried in vain to do for me in the past, when I had foolishly supposed my intelligence to be greater than hers. But as soon as we had gained more secluded surroundings I took no further part in her affairs. I did not look for dogs. I did not avoid them. It was up to her now, and she had her chances. Boxers, Labradors black and golden, Spaniels, mongrels, we had their company on various walks, sometimes singly, sometimes in groups.

And nothing ever happened. She flirted and played with them. They flew about together in high spirits. She stood for them from time to time. Nothing ever happened. Sometimes she stood in a perfunctory kind of way, sometimes with seeming purpose, lowering her rump. Sometimes they appeared to be on the mark, she would make her little protest and stand again. Often they clung to her in the unlikeliest places, even her head. She panted, they panted. Some were so exhausted by their efforts that they vomited, bringing up breakfast or lunch. Occasionally they fought among themselves. Fights, out of which, of course, Tulip herself freely skipped, were mostly started by some single dog with whom we had set out, objecting to interference from other dogs who joined us on the way. And this was understandable, but I was sorry nevertheless, the more so since the animals were disputing over something which none of them seemed able to possess. Indeed, now that I was a spectator merely, observing with detachment, I thought of them more deeply and regretted that I had added to canine social difficulties by my persecution of their fellows in the past. Not that I truly cared for them. Whatever breed or non-breed they might be, they seemed too preposterous or indistinct beside the wild beauty of my imperial bitch; but I saw how amiable and well-mannered they mostly were, in a way how sad, above all how nervous with their air of surreptitious guilt, and meeting the mild, worried brown eyes that often studied me and my friendly hand with doubt, I realized clearly, perhaps for the first time, what strained and anxious lives dogs must lead, so emotionally involved in the world of men, whose affections they strive endlessly to secure, whose authority they are expected unquestioningly to obey, and whose mind they never can do more than imperfectly reach and comprehend. Stupidly loved, stupidly hated, acquired without thought, reared and ruled without understanding, passed on or 'put to sleep' without care, did they, I wondered, these descendants of the creatures who, thousands of years ago in the primeval forests, laid siege to the heart of man, took him under their protection, tried to tame him, and failed—did they suffer from headaches?* Infinite pains I now took to reassure them, and sometimes succeeded. They perceived, after all, that, surprisingly enough, I did not mean to bully them or interfere; they saw too what a comradely relationship existed between myself and Tulip, whom I was always stooping down to caress and praise; in the end they would come confidently to meet me and put their cold noses against my hand.

But nothing ever happened. It was exactly the same as, excepting for Dusty, it always had been. And so convinced did I at last become that nothing ever would happen, that I no longer bothered to stop and wait for Tulip, or even to turn my head to see what kept her; soon, I knew, I would hear her protest and then she would come galloping after me, this grand lady with her entourage of inadequate wooers.

One day, late in her ninth year—the day, I afterwards understood, on which she would have whelped had a mating taken place—when she was sitting beside me in her armchair, she suddenly raised her hind leg and looked down at herself as if in dismay. A flux of bloody muck was oozing out of her. Like the birch tree she had her disease. She had gone bad inside. She had a septic womb.

* Tulip's skull is normally cool, but I have noticed that when she has undergone some agitating experience—a thunderstorm, a visit to the vet—her forehead gets quite hot.

. . .

This put an end to her sexual history, but not to her life. The irony of it all lay in my vet's information that it was a condition largely associated with non-breeding and usually found in elderly maiden bitches. This in-formation seems to provide an answer to the query in my footnote on page 128, though it leaves Tulip unex-plained. If the pus in the womb is able to escape, as in her case, the trouble can be quickly cleared up by hor-mone therapy. But not permanently. A recurrence is liable whenever the same point, the moment of parturi-tion, in the sexual cycle is reached. The wise course is to have the womb removed. Foolishly funking that (in the hands of a good surgeon the danger is slight), I chose therapy and the consequent worry of studying the calendar and keeping an anxious eye on Tulip whenever the biannual crises approached. For two-and-a-half years she lived ostensibly a perfectly normal, healthy life, though she could no longer be allowed to flirt with dogs in her seasons; then the muck streamed out again. Once more I funked surgery and had her treated; another two years passed without incident. At the age of fourteen her womb turned septic for the third time, therapy failed to control it, as I had been warned it might fail, and an emergency hysterectomy had to be performed. It was successful. Whatever blunders I may have committed in my management of this animal's life, she lived on to the great age of sixteen-and-a-half.

About the Author

J. R. Ackerley (1897–1976) was the literary editor of *The Listener,* the B.B.C. Magazine, from 1935 until 1959. He was a brilliant editor, tireless traveler and a prolific correspondent. His other books include *My Father and Myself, Hindoo Holiday,* and *We Think the World of You.* He lived most of his life in London.